My Friend Paul

My Friend Paul

An Intimate Walk with the Rabbi from Tarsus

DOUGLAS WARD

WIPF *&* STOCK · Eugene, Oregon

MY FRIEND PAUL
An Intimate Walk with the Rabbi from Tarsus

Copyright © 2023 Douglas Ward. All rights reserved. Except for brief quotations in critical publications or reviews, no part of this book may be reproduced in any manner without prior written permission from the publisher. Write: Permissions, Wipf and Stock Publishers, 199 W. 8th Ave., Suite 3, Eugene, OR 97401.

Wipf & Stock
An Imprint of Wipf and Stock Publishers
199 W. 8th Ave., Suite 3
Eugene, OR 97401

www.wipfandstock.com

PAPERBACK ISBN: 978-1-6667-7776-5
HARDCOVER ISBN: 978-1-6667-7777-2
EBOOK ISBN: 978-1-6667-7778-9

09/15/23

Scripture quotations marked (NIV) are taken from the Holy Bible, New International Version®, NIV®. Copyright © 1973, 1978, 1984 by Biblica, Inc.™ Used by permission of Zondervan. All rights reserved worldwide.

Contents

Introduction

There have been few people more influential in history than the man we know as Saul from Tarsus, or the apostle Paul. He authored more of the New Testament than any other author. While everyone agrees that Paul wrote seven of the twenty-seven books of the New Testament, many others would place that number at nine, ten, or even twelve books. His writings have been studied and examined in detail for centuries. Everyone knows the name Paul, but in many ways, he is a person still shrouded in history, and some of the things we "know" about Paul are probably little more than rumor, or poorly supported tradition. In reality, we know very little about this man, and we probably should study him much more than we have. If we take the time to learn about Paul a little more, we would certainly understand what he wrote better than we do. Here is the good news. If we pay attention to what he wrote about himself, there are enough hints for us to gain a clearer picture of this man named Paul.

I have studied Paul for most of my life. I feel like I know him. Yet he remains misunderstood, especially in the church. This is not a surprise as he was greatly misunderstood throughout his life by people in his own time. First, he was ostracized and misunderstood by the Jewish leaders of his day after his strange experience on the way to Damascus. To an even greater degree, he was distrusted by the leaders of the early church as well. For most of his adult life, Paul was a strong and scholarly man without a community to call his own. We think Paul was a leader of the early church, but he never assumed that role in the early church. Paul was the ultimate insider to the Jews in Jerusalem, who became an outsider worthy of arrest and imprisonment. To the early church Paul was deemed a dangerous man for his early persecution of Jewish believers, and his dangerous theological opinions later. At best he was a renegade leader who founded a rival expression of Christianity, and never gained the trust of the leaders of the early church. For most of his public life, Paul remained at odds with the leaders of the church in Jerusalem. Yet Paul's focus was not Jerusalem after his Damascus Road experience, and he traveled throughout the Roman Empire starting churches while the church in Jerusalem continued under the leadership of Peter and James. At the end of his life many of the churches he founded had turned against him and abandoned the gospel message he initially shared.

Paul lived a hard life. He went from early leader of the Jews to a renegade pest to both Jew and Christian alike. In his travels Paul battled Jesus' brother, and the former chief disciple throughout his journeys of Jesus' inner circle. As he preached Paul had to convince the believers why he was on the right side of history, while the highly regarded James and Peter were not. That understandably turned out to be a herculean task. He instructed libertines in Corinth, and stringent ascetics in Galatia. Sometimes the church listened to him, but most of the time they did not. He would even be "astonished" at how quickly some churches abandoned him. I think it was apparent that Paul was often frustrated and that he battled feelings of failure and constant disappointment throughout his journeys. Yet he persisted, struggled, and more importantly remained faithful. At the end of his impactful life Paul was able to look back at all the struggle and write, "I have finished the race. I have kept the faith." Because of this faithfulness Paul remains an important figure today.

Most of the time we read the words of Paul, bring his words forward to our own time, and start to discuss what these words mean to us. That process is like looking down on a city from a helicopter unaware of the conditions on the streets, and trying to determine what life is like on the ground. This will not be the approach of this book. I hope to take the reader to the ground level and walk with Paul in the first century, and in doing so explain not what Paul wrote, but why he wrote the words that he did. Hopefully this will be done in a way that every Christian can understand, so I hope to stay away from overly academic language and explain Paul to both the long-time Christian, or the new believer. At the end of this book, I hope both feel like they understand Paul better than at the beginning.

Hopefully, this book will introduce the reader to the man we know as Paul. We will look at history to understand his world and the unique forces that shaped his life and his views. We will also look at the words he wrote to help us understand Paul a little better. Some of these texts we know well. Other texts are more obscure to us. The words that Paul wrote will give us insight into this great, and driven man who risked everything to spread this newfound Jewish hope to the entire world, even to the steps of Rome. At the end my hope is that you will know this man better. I hope you will understand my friend Paul and the world in which he lived.

Saul of Tarsus
Leader of the Jews

We do not know much about Tarsus except for the fact that it is the hometown of my friend, Paul. We all know about the power and grandeur of Rome. Some of us know about the influence of the Egyptian city of Alexandria, but Tarsus is largely still a mystery. This is a shame because Tarsus was no provincial backwater. It was one of the leading cities of the Roman Empire and was situated in a highly important and strategic location. The city was located on the Cydnus River, which flowed through a highly fertile valley of Asia Minor. Although it was located roughly ten miles from the Mediterranean, ships were able to reach Tarsus via the river, making the city a prized port. Directly to the north of the city were the Cilician gates, a gorge through the Tarsus Mountains, through which ran the only good trade route between Asia Minor and the parts of the Empire to the east. Its economic importance was evident, and Paul himself was aware of its importance since in Acts 21:39 Paul admits he was from Tarsus, "a citizen of no mean city." Tarsus was important for other reasons as well. It became known as a city of great learning, perhaps rivaled only by Athens and Alexandria. Tarsus simply had almost everything that one would want in the Roman Empire—a thriving economic base and trade routes, an active philosophical community, and a permanent presence of the Roman army, making it very secure.

Tarsus had a history as well. Two generations prior, the Roman Empire was in the midst of a civil war. The forces of the leader who would be known as Augustus were struggling against the forces from the east under the leadership of Marc Antony. Looking to gain any advantage that he could, Antony summoned the Egyptian Queen Cleopatra to meet him in . . . Tarsus. Tarsus was the city where their famous love affair happened, and even though Antony and Cleopatra were ultimately defeated, Tarsus retained a permanent presence of the Roman army. Since a significant part of this revolt was centered around Tarsus, it seemed good to Rome to keep forces stationed there to prevent another one. If another civil war would gain traction in Rome, it would not come from Tarsus, the place where the prior one had gained steam. An army would have needed resources, and there were few places better than Tarsus. Its fertile land, strategic location along trade routes, and its navigable port made it the perfect location to support an army, while enabling the army to quickly go to locations in the eastern part of the Empire. While Tarsus was in Asia Minor, it was a city thoroughly intertwined with every strand of the powerful and prosperous Roman Empire.

This is the first part of the story that helps illuminate the life of Paul. We know from the New Testament that Paul's trade was tent-making. In that day one did not go to trade school and choose your trade, but one simply inherited the trade and livelihood of the family. In all likelihood, Paul learned how to make tents by watching his father make tents. Tent-making would have been a valuable trade in Tarsus, more valuable than in most other cities. While a tent-maker might have made a living almost anywhere, a city which housed a permanent garrison of the Roman army would have valued a tent-maker even more. Whenever the Roman army went on the march, they would have needed tents for shelter in the field. As a tent-making resident in Tarsus, it seems highly plausible that Paul's father made tents for travelers, citizens, and probably made tents for the Roman army.

One of the enduring mysteries of the New Testament is trying to figure out how Paul was a Roman citizen. The overwhelming majority of people living in the Roman Empire were not citizens. Most people who lived in Rome were classified as slaves, and others were simply laborers, doing their best to make a living. The question is, how did Paul get to be a citizen in a time when they did not pass out citizenship freely? The easiest answer is that Paul's father must have been a citizen, and the most likely route of that citizenship is to have done a service for Rome, or her army. It is not a stretch at all to conclude that a tent-maker would have served Rome by making tents for her armies. After connecting the dots available to us we can reasonably conclude that Paul was a citizen of Rome because his dad had made tents for the Roman army and was granted citizenship as a reward for that service. As a son of a citizen, Paul was a citizen as well. Ironically, the philosophy that Paul would later espouse would be considered a threat by the same Rome that conferred citizenship on Paul's father only a generation earlier. Toward the end of his life as he sat in a Roman prison, that irony was not lost on Paul.

Tarsus was also home to a thriving Jewish community. The Jews thrived in Tarsus, and it would not have been rare for a Jewish family to seek specialized education for some of their sons. Apparently, Paul's family was one of those thriving families, and they sent their son to study Judaism under the guidance of Gemaliel in Jerusalem. While this is an obscure name to us, Gemaliel was anything but obscure in the first century. His grandfather was Rabbi Hillel, perhaps the most influential Jewish teacher of his, or any other day. This family lineage to Hillel would have made this type of religious training not only valued, but also very prestigious for any family who wanted the best for their son. Paul would not have been seen as an average Jew in his day, but one with a highly esteemed pedigree.

In the first century there were two dominant sects of Judaism: the Pharisees and the Sadducees. The Sadducees were the conservative and powerful wing of Judaism. Allied with Rome, they were largely in control of the temple and the power structures of Judaism within Jerusalem. The Sadducees did not believe in the resurrection, and only considered the words of the Torah authoritative. When it came to the other writings and teachings within Judaism, the Sadducees did not consider them worthy of esteem or reverence. To rank and file Jews, the Sadducees were the Jews who were ensconced in the ivory towers of the first century, disconnected from the people and the struggle of their everyday lives. They were distant from the average Jewish family and were not highly esteemed.

The other dominant wing of Judaism was the Pharisees. We tend to think of them as the bad guys of the gospels, but this would not be accurate. The Pharisees were very popular to the average Jews of the first century, especially the Pharisees who followed the teachings of Rabbi Hillel. They were considered innovative, people-friendly, and tried to make Judaism accessible to the masses. The average Jew of the first century may have asked, "What does it mean to honor the Sabbath?" The Pharisees would have responded with a series of expectations and rules that described in detail what it meant to honor the Sabbath day. We view it as excessive and restrictive, primarily because of Matthew's gospel, but to the Jews of the first century, such instructions were helpful. If a person wanted to know how to keep the law as a faithful Jew, having a list of expectations would have been welcome. The Pharisees under Rabbi Hillel were popular and seen positively by the people. Hillel tried to make Judaism accessible to the people and was the figure who tried to keep the ancient faith connected to the average lives of the people. Now the grandson of that great Rabbi would be chosen to teach the exceptionally bright student from Tarsus named Paul.

We have no record or traditions about what Paul was like as a student, but it is not hard to imagine. Paul was a student that enthusiastically embraced his Jewish heritage and his studies. It seems he was a driven student. In his own words he proclaimed that he advanced in Judaism beyond his peers. It is hard to imagine such a statement about a sloppy or disconnected student. He also described himself as zealous about his Judaism.

> If someone else thinks they have reasons to put confidence in the flesh, I have more: circumcised on the eighth day, of the people of Israel, of the tribe of Benjamin, a Hebrew of Hebrews; in regard to the law, a Pharisee; as for

> zeal, persecuting the church; as for righteousness based
> on the law, faultless. (Phil 3:3–6, NIV)

Paul was out to prove something, and he took his Judaism seriously.

One wonders if his childhood in Tarsus made a deep impression on the young Paul. Paul would have been raised with the normal level of Jewish expectations. He would have known the Scriptures, he would have been hopeful for a coming Messiah, and he would have longed for the coming age when the Messiah would defeat the enemies of Israel and establish a just and lasting kingdom. When that day comes Israel would assume its rightful place, and empires like Rome would no longer have prominence. Thoughts of the coming Messiah and his kingdom inspired the young Paul, then Paul would help his dad deliver the tents they had made to the army that carried out the wishes of Rome. I think the young Paul seethed inwardly with each delivery. Then Paul carried those experiences with him to Jerusalem and his studies and used them to fuel his efforts. His superiors noticed this intense and zealous student and gave him ever-increasing responsibilities. Paul surpassed their expectations with each task, and he became a prominent Pharisee, even as a young man.

As Paul studied the words contained in the Jewish Scriptures these words became second nature to him. He longed for the Messiah who would defeat the enemies of Israel, and then rule in peace like described in Zechariah 9. That would be the time when the Spirit would be poured out on all flesh (Joel 2), and then no longer will there be a need for teachers because all of Israel will know their God (Jer 31). Until that time Israel was called to be faithful. Paul took that call seriously, and even if no one else in Israel would be faithful, Paul would be. As far as it depended on Paul, he was going to keep every single rule contained in the law. Many believers today mistakenly think that Jews of Paul's time strived to keep the law in an effort to earn a certain status before God, but this was not the case. This was not how a Jew obtained salvation, because every Jew knew they did not earn their "chosen" status—they were simply chosen by God. Their status was not a result of their choice, but was a result of God's choice. They kept the law to remain in the covenant and as a result keep their promised land. Paul was a Jew's Jew, and he would keep every rule. This is a task that Paul did perfectly, and he admitted such in Philippians 3. When it came to keeping all the rules, Paul was blameless. Such a young man was certainly serious about his Judaism.

There is one other question that has dogged the study of the youthful Paul, and that is whether or not Paul was married. The prevailing opinion has always been that Paul was not married, but that opinion is premature, and probably mistaken. It is true that we have no proof that Paul was married, but it should be noted that we also have no proof that he was single either. What we do have is the well-established cultural expectation that Jewish men should be married. This was more than just an expectation, but a vital commitment for a Jewish male, especially one that had goals to rise through the ranks of Jewish leadership. It is nearly impossible to imagine that a man who expected to be a leader within Judaism would not be married. When one looks at the ambition and goals that Paul fostered, it seems evident that Paul would have been married on the basis of cultural expectations alone.

It is true that it seems that Paul was single by the time he wrote his letters to the church in Corinth. Yet we should not make the mistake of ascribing his later status to all of his earlier years. We should remember that Paul lived in a time when influenza was often deadly and a third of women died in childbirth. We do not know the details of his earlier life, but it seems probable that Paul married, even as it seems evident that by the time of his later ministry, this wife was no longer a part of Paul's life. The most logical conclusion we can reach is that Paul had been married at one time, but his wife had died an early death.

While we cannot state with certainty what Paul looked like, we do have a description in an apocryphal book called *The Acts of Paul and Thecla,* where Paul is described: "he was a man of middling size, and his hair was scanty, and his legs were a little crooked, and his knees were projecting, and he had large eyes. His eyebrows met, his nose was somewhat long, and he was full of grace and mercy. At one time he seemed like a man, and at another time he seemed like an angel."[1] There are problems with this description as this work is usually dated to the late second century, meaning considerable time has passed before this physical description. There was also the ancient tendency to associate certain moral or personality traits with a physical trait. We do not know if Paul is being physically described with these words, or if this is a character description. However, it should be noted that in ancient paintings Paul often fits this description quite well.

Some might be reading this and wondering why I am using the name Paul instead of the name we read when we first encounter Paul—Saul. There are many who mistakenly believe that Saul was his name, and then at some point his name changed to Paul. Others go even further and state that God changed his name from Saul to Paul upon his conversion experience. Neither of these is true. The simple truth is that Saul was always Paul's name, and Paul was always Saul's name. if you think this makes no sense, let me explain what I mean.

Paul was a citizen of Rome. A citizen of Rome would have a tribal name, which in Paul's case would have been his Jewish name, a Roman name, and then the place of his birth. Thus, Paul's name was Saulus Paulus of Tarsus. This would have been Paul's name for his entire life. Early in Acts when Paul is in Judea, it should come as no surprise that he is called Saul. When Paul is on his missionary journeys, he is uniformly called Paul, not because his name has changed post-conversion, but because he is outside of Judea, so his Roman name would have been used. Later, when Paul returns to Jerusalem in Acts 21, notice that he is called Saul again. There was never a name change, just the use of the name that matched where he was within the Roman Empire. The modern reader misses this, but the first readers of Acts would have intuitively known this.

Finally, there is one other part of Paul's life that is commonly misunderstood. Most Christians think that Paul routinely killed Christians as a part of his life as a Jewish leader. We popularly describe Paul as one who traveled around looking for Christians to kill. This is understandable in light of Acts 7 where the cloaks of

---

1 *Acts of Paul and Thecla* 1:7.

those who stoned Stephen were laid at the feet of a young Paul. This is taken as proof that Paul killed Christians. There is one large problem with this view of Paul—Rome. It was not that Rome was against capital punishment since they routinely put thousands of people to death. It was the ultimate demonstration of Roman power over the lives of its citizens. You go against us and we will put you to death. That was their threat, and it was a threat Rome carried out with impunity. This was aptly demonstrated just one hundred years prior when over six thousand slaves who participated in the rebellion led by Spartacus were crucified at the same time. The problem was that Rome was the only power that executed people, and Rome jealously guarded that right for themselves alone. In fact, if you wanted the attention of Rome, execute people without their permission and you would have had it. Paul did not have the authority to put anyone to death. Whatever authority Paul was granted by Jewish leaders extended only to discipline those within the Jewish synagogue.

This still leads us back to the deadly event with Stephen in Acts 7. We simply do not know exactly what is being described in this passage. Was it an event that Paul authorized somehow, with the hope that Rome would not notice? That is certainly possible. The stoning of Stephen could have also been a mob action where Paul was simply present. Paul might have been there in the capacity to check on the dangerous words of this upstart preacher, and when the mob turned against Stephen, Paul could have simply watched. He might have quietly approved of the action while not authorizing the activity directly. It is also possible that Luke uses this event to cast Paul in a specific light. Here is a Christian being killed by a Jewish mob, and in the middle of this mob is this intense Jew named Paul.

While we do not know the exact relationship of Paul with the killers of Stephen, we do have a pretty good sketch of Paul before what is commonly called his conversion. He was a confident and determined man, who desired to rise to the top of the ranks of the Jewish leadership. He was also unique in ways that very few others were. He was a highly educated Roman citizen who was comfortable in the temple, or the halls discussing the philosophies of Greece and Rome. Yet he was proud of his Jewish heritage and wanted to keep the Judaism of his day correct and pure. All the while he awaited the Messiah, and the coming age when God would make everything right. As Paul was rising through the ranks of Judaism a group of people started to swell the ranks within Judaism. They claimed the Messiah had arrived and told a strange story of death and resurrection. This now risen Messiah had even died on a cross. This was simply unacceptable to Paul, and almost all of his contemporary Pharisees. The book of Deuteronomy was clear that anyone hung on a tree was considered cursed (Deut 21:23). This "cursed" Messiah was an idea that had to be eliminated, and Paul was given the task of dealing with it. In pursuit of this dangerous idea, Paul was sent to Syria to confront some in the synagogue there. This was the life Paul had chosen and pursued and was pursuing that day on his way to Damascus. The trip to Damascus would have been a difficult journey, but it was a journey that was worth the effort. Paul had prepared to be a man of influence from the time of his youth and there needed to be a change in Damascus. Paul was the perfect man to be the catalyst for change in Damascus, but it was not the change my friend Paul had planned.

The Road
The Day Everything Changed

The trip to Damascus was not much different than other trips Paul had undertaken. First there were reports of some causing a commotion in the synagogue in Damascus. Trouble was nothing new for Jewish communities, but lately the trouble seemed to center on this person Jesus. There were some in Damascus who were claiming that this Jesus was not only the Messiah, but was God himself in the flesh. Because of this potential trouble Paul was sent to evaluate the problem and, if necessary, bring the agitators back to Jerusalem for trial.

Paul and his companions set out on the road to Damascus, and there was nothing unusual about the trip—just too many miles on an arid and dusty road. There was nothing outside of the ordinary that happened on this trip until that completely strange and unexpected event early in the afternoon. One minute Paul was walking along the road, and the next minute he was lying on the ground talking to. . .. no one in particular; at least it seemed that way to Paul's companions. His companions immediately worried that Paul might be losing his mind. After all, how often does someone just collapse and start holding a strained conversation with a person no one else could see? His companions heard the anguished Paul mutter into the air, "Who are you, Lord?" Even more concerning was the abrupt change in Paul's physical condition. He was not only talking gibberish to an unseen person, but suddenly he could no longer see.

In our day our first thought would be to get Paul to a hospital and do a complete examination. There would be CT scans, or MRIs in an effort to detect a possible physical cause. This would not have been the case in the first century. Blindness, as well as many other physical maladies, was considered to be the result of a lack of favor from God. If these maladies also had someone speaking gibberish into the air, this might be the result of an evil spirit. For Paul, this was not only a physical malady, but one with spiritual overtones that threatened his standing in the Jewish community he helped lead. Taking pity on him, Paul's friends helped him to his feet, and guided him personally all the way to Damascus, even as they wondered what had happened to their dedicated persecutor, and what would become of him in the future.

Whatever his companions experienced, the event on the road was even more searing and confusing for Paul. The physical impact alone would have been overwhelming for anyone. Paul was in the prime of his life, and on his way to the top of Jewish religious and political influence. His trusted standing in the community led the leaders to trust him with the task of keeping the belief and practice of the community correct. He was pursuing this goal like he had done many times before. Then in the space of seconds he became blind and dependent upon friends to get him to Damascus. Life was suddenly and completely upended.

Perhaps more than the physical, Paul's religious world was turned upside down as well. Paul had been committed to forcibly retaining the correct understanding of Jewish thought, and the great agitators had been those Jews who followed that disgraced criminal—Jesus Christ. It was a simple equation, except this Jesus had somehow just appeared to Paul amid the mid-day sun, challenged him, and left him blinded. Even if this episode turned out to be some false, half-crazy experience, this blindness alone could easily serve to derail all his future plans and goals. In hindsight we talk glowingly of Paul's experience on the road to Damascus. Yet for Paul this was a disruptive and shattering experience that completely upended his life. Everything that Paul had worked his entire life to attain was gone in a second. His life would never be the same again. For most of us we associate turning to Christ with the assumption that life will get better, and more blessed. This was simply not the case with Paul. He had an experience with Christ and his life not only got harder, but became what most would consider worse.

Part of the struggle for Paul was that he did not even have the language to describe what had happened to him on that road. It was a completely unexpected and unprecedented event. How would he ever be able to tell people about this experience? As a Pharisee, Paul looked forward to the resurrection in the last days. He really believed that God would intervene and set things right. Yet how would he ever describe this; Jesus, the one whom Paul worked so hard to counteract, had appeared to him! As a Jew, Paul believed and expected that there would be a future resurrection. The problem with these believers in Jesus was that they claimed the resurrection had already happened, and Jesus was alive. Paul was trying to end this belief, but this Jesus was the person he saw and experienced on the dusty road. If this experience was real then the resurrection did not happen at the end of history as he previously believed, but it happened in the middle of history—Paul's and Israel's history. If what he saw and heard was true, then everything would have to be reconsidered. This was more than just an intense experience, and it was more than suddenly becoming blind, this event shattered every paradigm Paul thought he knew. So how could he ever describe it?

This was what bewildered Paul. These disruptive, Jewish believers made the ridiculous claim they had seen Jesus—a crucified man alive. On the way to rid Jewish believers of this delusion, Paul had seen the same man. There were no words for this experience.

Paul tried to explain it in 2 Cor 12:2–4. He said:

> I know a man in Christ who fourteen years ago was caught up to the third heaven. Whether it was in the body or out of the body I do not know—God knows. And I know that this man—whether in the body or apart from the body I do not know, but God knows—was caught up to

paradise and heard inexpressible things, things that no
one is permitted to tell." (NIV)

While it is not immediately apparent, this passage of Corinthians refers to Paul himself. This is difficult language to understand, because it is not language that we hear every day, but it is
important to hear what Paul is saying here. In the Jewish worldview
the world was composed of three, or sometimes seven, heavenly
layers. We should think of layers of an onion as a model here. The
first layer is where humanity lives and moves, the second layer was
composed of great waters, being held back by God in preparation
for judgment. The third layer, or the third through seventh layers, are where the angels, archangels, and God himself dwells. We
should remember this is not a scientific view, but a pre-scientific
view of the world. Therefore, when Paul says he was caught up to
the third heaven, it is a way of saying that he cannot describe what
happened to him. It was an event too awe-inspiring for words. Paul
knew he had seen Jesus, and he could not tell you if he saw Jesus
physically, or in some great vision beyond this reality, but this encounter had been real, even though he could not quite put it into
words.

Something had happened to Paul on that dusty road in the
noon-day sun, and it had changed Paul's life forever. Yet how should
we describe what happened to Paul? For years the dominant word
has been that this was Paul's conversion, yet that word does not
seem to fit this experience well. Before the Damascus Road Paul
had been a zealous follower of God who strived to be faithful and
obedient while teaching others to live in the same manner. This
exact description also fits Paul perfectly after his experience on
the way to Damascus. Paul claimed he was blameless before the
Damascus Road, and he strived to live that way after still. So "conversion" does not seem quite right. His religious commitment was
almost total both before and after the trip to Damascus. It is also
clear from his letters that Paul considered himself a Jew both before and after the Damascus Road. If conversion is the right word
for this experience, then what did Paul convert to?

Other people have recently started to use the word "call" to describe the change Paul experienced. Before the Damascus Road Paul had spent his life serving the family of God, which according to his understanding were the Jews. After the road to Damascus, Paul still strived to serve God's people, only his understanding of that group had now widened. He now had been "called" to reach the gentiles. This description seems logical but somehow seems to minimize the impact of what happened to Paul on that day. If conversion is not the right word, call seems to be too limited in scope. Perhaps what happened to Paul was a complete re-orientation.

This re-orientation was widespread. The focus of Paul's efforts changed. He still followed the Jewish God, but his understanding of that God was completely different. His companions changed. His commitment to the Scriptures was identical, but what those words meant had turned around. He once sought to imprison others who did not share his views, but now Paul was a candidate for arrest and persecution himself. Everything had changed, and words to describe that change are hard to find.

Yet we also must admit that we do not know much about this part of Paul's story, and this is a key point of Paul's life. We know that Paul saw Ananais, regained his sight, and that he spent time with the believers in Damascus, but we have no idea what happened to the men who traveled with Paul. We may have hints in Acts 9 when we read that the Jews were so enraged by Paul that they sought to kill him. This part of the story is subject to some of the same troubles that we read in the Stephen story—that Jews did not have the authority to kill under the umbrella of Rome. Yet the tension with his former Jewish companions was acute. We also do not know why Paul was the object of their anger. Was it failure to complete the mission? Was it disappointment with a Paul who abandoned the particular Pharisaical expression of Judaism? Or was it his embrace of the Christian message? Perhaps it was a combination of all three. We just know that Paul's life and trajectory had changed forever and this change complicated Paul's life immensely.

In many ways these years became the most difficult of Paul's life, and we do not appreciate the trial that Paul endured here. Paul had spent his entire adult life, from the age of thirteen to this moment, pursuing the rigors of Jewish life, and advancing within the leadership of the Pharisees. By every measure Paul was an ambitious and driven man. His own words indicate the amount of pride and confidence Paul had in his life and efforts to follow God. Whatever this event was on the Damascus Road, Paul was now ostracized from his own people, at least the ones in leadership.

One might think that Paul naturally gravitated toward the Christians, but that is not what happened. Paul escaped from Damascus and returned to Jerusalem. While there he tried to join the believers, but initially they shunned Paul. This is a natural reaction to one who just weeks earlier had been trying to discipline these early Christians. They thought it was all a ploy to infiltrate the church and do harm to the believers. Finally, Barnabas intervened and personally vouched for Paul and took him to meet the disciples. Acts tells us the meeting happened, but the Jews were still angry with Paul, so he is sent to Tarsus for his own safety.

Here is where it might be good to read between the lines in Acts. While Acts does not explicitly tell us, it seems obvious that all is still not smooth between Paul and the disciples in Jerusalem. The events surrounding Paul's conversion/call experience happened around AD 30 to 34. Twelve to fifteen years later, Paul was still not in Jerusalem and was connected with the church meeting in Antioch. Still not seemingly welcome in Jerusalem, Paul was not active in the church led by Peter, and James, Jesus' brother. Paul eventually spent more than a decade on the sidelines. He was alienated from the Jewish leadership, and obviously mistrusted by the church. Paul was a man without a people. He was utterly alone.

These were the toughest years for Paul. In years to come he would be arrested, beaten, imprisoned, and shipwrecked, but Paul was a man who was built for the conflict. Those days were not easy, but they were days of impact. They were days when Paul would be heard, and he could present his ideas among friends and opponents. Paul loved the ideas and loved to make an argument. The hardest thing for Paul was to do nothing, and to be idle in the arena of ideas. Those years were tough. He had so much to say, but no one to say it to, and no one really trusted him.

Something changed around the year AD 47. Acts is silent on the matter, and we are not sure why, but Paul is sent on his first missionary journey. We should notice that Paul is sent by the church in Antioch, and not by the church in Jerusalem. We know there is still mistrust because when the church in Jerusalem hears that Paul is out preaching, they dispatch people to follow in Paul's footsteps, and correct the message that Paul has proclaimed.While we celebrate Paul's initial success with his mission, the church in Jerusalem certainly did not celebrate. In fact, they sent people after Paul in an attempt to counter part of Paul's message.

We are not sure why initially, but Paul finds success reaching the gentiles in Galatia. We do not know if Paul was ignored by the Jews, or whether his initial efforts were to reach out to the gentiles, but it is the gentiles who respond. Paul has success, but that success immediately causes problems. The Jews have spent centuries separating themselves from the gentiles in virtually every area of life. Now that gentiles were responding to the Jewish God, what role would they have as part of God's people? The Jews allowed people to convert to Judaism, but these converts were expected to embrace the Jewish way of life. That expectation remained, even with the new, Christian faith of these Jews. Most of the Jews expected these new gentile believers to embrace these same Jewish customs.

The issue comes to a head rapidly. Paul has returned from his first journey, and Peter has joined him in Antioch. Paul spends the meeting introducing Peter to these new believers, and the new customs of this gentile church. What follows is one of the most riveting stories in Scripture. Peter has joined Paul for a communal meal with the Gentiles. Peter joins Paul, eats with the Gentiles, and is a part of the community until men representing the Jerusalem church arrive. Peter sees the arrival of these men and withdraws from the table and fellowship with these new believers, and Paul is incensed. One can imagine Paul and Peter sitting at a meal catered by Famous Daves in Antioch, enjoying the barbecue with the little plastic bibs on, when Peter looks up and sees representatives arrive from Jerusalem. Peter jumps up, yanks off his bib, and quickly wipes his hands with the lemon scented wet-nap to remove the smell. Peter then rushes over to greet these men from Jerusalem, who represent the church there, and its leader, James, the brother of Jesus.

While this presentation of the event is meant to be humorous, it captures the importance of that event. Paul and Jerusalem are not on good terms. There is a real division between what Paul is doing, and what the church in Jerusalem does. There is much that hangs in the balance, and the future of the new, Christian church is at stake. It is easy to underestimate the consequences of this dispute. Whether this Christianity becomes a world-wide faith now hangs in the balance. If Paul does not prevail, then Christianity will stay just a small sect of Judaism. Paul's opponents expect Christianity to stay as a sect of Judaism, and they find no problem with that outcome. Most people present there would have no problem with this outcome. There was only one person who saw the danger, and that was my friend, Paul.

That is an ironic statement since Paul was the zealous, Jewish leader, and ex-Pharisee. All of the odds were stacked against Paul from the beginning. After all, the people on the other side of the argument were Peter, the famed disciple, and James, Jesus' brother. It was natural to believe them. Why would anyone believe Paul, especially with his history? We underestimate the nature of this early struggle in the church. Paul, the early persecutor, is preaching a message of justification by faith alone. Standing against him were Peter, the close disciple of Jesus, and Jesus' brother James. Paul tries to convince the early believers that he was right, while Peter and James were misguided. It was a real struggle that did not go well, but Paul did not give up. We should not forget how much of a struggle it was for my friend, Paul.

The Revolution
Salvation By Faith

As a faithful Jew, Paul knew the Scriptures well, and what the coming kingdom of God would look like. After spending thirteen to fifteen years in obscurity following his Damascus Road experience, Paul was preaching in Asia Minor, and his efforts were finally paying off in Galatia. Gentiles were responding to his message, and were publicly following the Jewish God made flesh, Jesus Christ. The question was, how could Paul integrate these gentiles into a faith that was almost entirely comprised of Jews?

Fortunately for Paul, his Damascus Road experience had completely changed his life, and forced him to completely re-orient his thinking. Perhaps the most surprising thing about his ordeal was that his beloved law had nothing to do with what had happened to him. Paul had dedicated his life to upholding the law, but whatever happened to him on that road had nothing to do with the precepts he had studied his whole life. He had followed the letter of the law for a lifetime, and it did not change him on the inside. What did change him was an unscheduled encounter with an unlikely resurrected Messiah on that dusty road. This surprising event forced Paul to reconsider many of his base assumptions about what was important.

Paul's eyes were opened even further in Galatia. There were moments when Paul doubted what had happened to him. The results of that encounter had changed his life immeasurably, and at times it was unclear whether it was for the better. For the first thirteen years or so of his Christian life, that encounter had diminished Paul and his place in the world. Then, in Galatia he personally witnessed these Gentiles have a similar experience to his. How could it be that these pagan gentiles were experiencing God in the same manner that he had? Even though he was a pious Jew and these Galatians were Gentile, they shared one very prominent trait in common—the law did not factor into either of their religious experiences. As a result, Paul was forced to search for the common denominator between not only himself and these new gentiles, but all who had experienced Christ. Fortunately for Paul he did not have to look far. He found it in his beloved Old Testament and Habakkuk 2—the righteous will live by faith. Through his experience Paul was forced to admit that we come to Christ through this faith, not through his former practice of observing the law.

When Paul arrived in a community for the first time, he preached a very simple message. It derived from the story of Abraham and his encounter with God in Genesis 15. Paul's logic was simple, and it flowed through much of his letter-writing in the New Testament. Abraham encountered God, and God asked Abraham to trust him, and obey his call. God told Abraham, "Go to a land I will show you." The point of the Old Testament story was that Abraham obeyed God and uprooted his family in obedience to God. Genesis 15:6 then makes the following statement that undergirds Paul's argument: "Abraham believed God, and it was credited to him as righteousness."

This story quickly became the focal point for everything that Paul said. While the law had been the centerpiece of his life, Paul now realized the law could not have made Abraham righteous, since it would not even be given for another four hundred years. What established Abraham in God's sight was his simple trust in the words of God. Paul had responded to the vision and words of Christ, and now the Gentiles were doing the same thing through the ministry of Paul. This is how the new family of God would be constituted—simple faith. This had the added benefit of not even being a new standard for it had existed within Judaism for centuries. This simple faith had eventually become hidden by external adherence to the law. Paul now realized that God's people had always lived by faith, whether they are Abraham's family centuries prior, or brand-new gentile believers in Galatia.

This was a new and unexpected expression of membership into the family of God that Paul has developed. Jew and Gentile, slave and free are granted equal status into the churches he has established. While this seems like good news, the church leaders in Jerusalem did not take this news well. Instead of celebrating the establishment of these new churches, they were threatened by the foundations that Paul was establishing. Upon hearing the news of Paul's activities, they sent representatives of their own to the churches that Paul had established. These men came to the churches Paul founded and preached strongly from Genesis 17—the familiar Jewish maxim that every male among you must be circumcised. Paul was a great guy, they proclaimed, but he only told you half of the story. Yes, we come to Christ in faith, but in order to be God's people we are bound to keep the law, and this includes these gentile believers. Their instruction was you must keep the food laws, observe the special days, and submit to the covenant of circumcision, the Jewish representatives said. In their zeal to embrace this new faith, the gentile Galatians willingly submitted to these age-old Jewish practices.

This is the heart of the disagreement we find in Galatians 2:15–21. This is a well-known passage to us, and is one of the most quoted passages in Protestant circles.

> We who are Jews by birth and not sinful gentiles know that a person is not justified by the works of the law, but by faith in Jesus Christ. So we, too, have put our faith in Christ Jesus that we may be justified by faith in Christ and not by the works of the law, because by the works of the law no one will be justified. (Gal 2:15–16, NIV)

Modern believers read this passage through the lens we have inherited from Martin Luther. As a result, we think Paul is describing good works in this passage. Yet this is not the case. The phrase "works of the law" was a technical phrase in the first century. It did not mean meritorious deeds, but those things a Jew did to remain in the covenant and be seen by others as a Jew. No Jew thought in terms of earning their status, they received their status straight from God, and did not need to qualify for that status. They kept the law to remain in the covenant.

There is one other part of this passage that many have failed to appreciate, and that is the phrase "faith in Jesus Christ." In recent years a convincing case has been made that this is not the best translation. It should be translated "faith of Jesus Christ," or "the faithfulness of Christ." This not only makes a huge difference in how we read Galatians, but it has the added benefit of clearing up Paul's meaning in Galatians. Instead, it should read, we are "not justified by observing the works of the law, but through the faithfulness of Jesus Christ." This is an important distinction. In the former reading faith is turned into an act that we do. In this second reading, the grounds for our salvation are firmly planted in the historical event of Jesus on the cross.

When we read this phrase, it is clear that Paul has returned to his Jewish Scriptures once again. After the promise to Abraham, God and Abraham established a covenant together. In the custom of their day a number of animals are sacrificed and laid side by side. Both parties then are supposed to walk between these animals together, and in doing so agree that if either of them breaks their agreement, may what happened to these animals happen to them. At the last minute though, God causes Abraham to fall into a deep sleep, and God walks through the sacrificed animals alone. In doing so God stated that if either party violates this agreement, I will be the one who bears the penalty alone. When Jesus goes to the cross, God is being faithful to the covenant he made with Abraham. Instead of faith becoming an act for us to do, faithfulness is the willing decision Jesus made in our behalf. None of us have ever been saved by a decision that we made. We are all saved by what Christ did, and that is why this faith is not solely a Jewish possession. Paul grounded our salvation into what Christ did, not what we do.

With Paul's success gaining new converts to the faith a new battle had developed, whether in Galatia over circumcision, or

Corinth over the eating of idol meat. The battle was theological, and it centered over who was a better interpreter of the Old Testament. The Jewish-Christians, with some new Gentiles also holding to the traditional expressions of Judaism, or the former leader of the Pharisees, Paul, pleading with the church that gentiles should not be forced to follow the Jewish law at all, since simple faith is the new marker for the people of God.

Many Christians today fundamentally misread the point that Paul made so consistently. We look back at Paul's instruction and think that Paul is making a faith versus good works argument. You are saved by faith and not by doing good works, because no one can earn salvation through the doing of good works. It is all grace. While we agree that salvation is by grace, Paul is not constructing a dichotomy between faith and good works in his letters. Faith versus works is a modern argument, largely coming from the times and setting of Martin Luther, but it was not an argument that any Jew in the first century would have made. It is simply foreign to the worldview of Paul.

If one were a Jew in the first century, they would not have thought it was possible to earn their status as part of God's family by keeping the law. A Jew was "chosen" not because they obeyed the law, they were simply chosen because they were Jews. A Jew was a part of God's people the moment they were born, and nothing they did earned this special status. A Jew was obedient to the law in order to keep and protect their status as God's people. In an effort to accomplish this, Jews observed the food laws, submitted to circumcision, and observed the ceremonies. This effort was not a quest to gain a new status before God, but to keep the status they had due to God's choice.

We think that Jews kept the law as a currency to use to gain this special status. Instead, it was an identity badge, used to physically mark out a special people as different from everyone else. Jews were God's family. The question was, who is a Jew? It is one who did all the things the law requires. One kept the law to mark themselves as different from the peoples around them. Into this background came these new believers that Paul had convinced.

Paul even called them a part of God's family. When the Jewish Christians heard this claim, many of them resisted. "Wait a minute," they protested, "if I had to get circumcised, so does Titus. If I could never eat pork, then neither can you." They were not against the inclusion of these new people, but they were against them being considered a part of the church on Paul's brand-new terms. They can become a part of the church, the Jewish believers claimed, but it has to be on our terms. And those terms are spelled out in Genesis 17. This new church was not twenty years old yet, and a critical impasse had already been reached. The outcome of this impasse would determine the direction of this new church.

When one considers all of the issues that were present in the world of the first century, it is hard to imagine why circumcision and pork would rise to the top of the list, but yet it had. Believe it or not the Old Testament had led Paul to this viewpoint. Something was happening, and God was doing something totally unexpected. The other Jewish leaders were having difficulty explaining this phenomenon, but for the Paul, the trained Pharisee, the Scripture could not have been clearer. The prophet Joel had written words centuries earlier that seemed to fit Paul's day perfectly. "And afterward, I will pour out my Spirit on all people. Your sons and daughters will prophesy, your old men will dream dreams, your young men will see visions" (Joel 2:28). So too had the prophet Jeremiah in chapter 31 when he wrote, "This is the covenant I will make with the people of Israel after that time," declares the Lord. "I will put my law in their minds and write it on their hearts. I will be their God, and they will be my people"(Jer 31:33). These ancient texts crystallized in the mind of Paul. If one was against what God was doing in the lives of these new gentile converts, it would not be going against a new trend, but against what God had stated he would do centuries earlier. Paul was not shedding his Jewish heritage to come to this conclusion, rather his heritage was leading him directly to this position.

The leaders of this new Christian movement needed to settle this issue, so they sent leaders to meet in Jerusalem. Paul was back from his first journey, and he met with the leadership of the church in Jerusalem. The leaders of this new church met to decide the fate of these new believers. The question was twofold, would they be allowed into the church, and if so, what would be their requirements for membership? There was the dominant faction of the church, represented by James, and was headquartered in Jerusalem. On the other side was the upstart Paul, flush with his recent success of adding many gentile converts to Christianity. The meeting was intense, and neither side was willing to give too much ground. The Jewish believers had centuries of tradition on their side, and Paul had these new converts and churches on his, along with the certainty his intellect and training provided him. Much hung in the balance. Without a doubt this meeting could have ended in a variety of different ways, and the future of the church would look different under each scenario.

In Acts 15, Luke gives us a compelling story. There is great agreement among the participants of the conference. The agreement is not only great, but Luke throws in the word unanimous in verse 25 to make it sound all the more triumphant. He writes,

> We have heard that some went out from us without our authorization and disturbed you, troubling your minds by what they said. So we all agreed to choose some men and send them to you with our dear friends Barnabas and Paul—men who have risked their lives for the name of our Lord Jesus Christ. Therefore we are sending Judas and Silas to confirm by word of mouth what we are writing. It seemed good to the Holy Spirit and to us not to burden you with anything beyond the following requirements: You are to abstain from food sacrificed to idols, from blood, from the meat of strangled animals and from sexual immorality. You will do well to avoid these things." (Acts 15:24–28, NIV)

The news would seem to be good. The Gentiles are allowed into the church. When one considers the identity of God's people, now the gentiles will also be a part of that group. Even better, there is not much that is going to be asked of them. With just a few requirements, the Gentiles will be granted full status in the fledgling church. All they have to do is keep kosher with the meat they eat, avoid sexual immorality, and refrain from eating meat that has been sacrificed to idols. This is not too much to ask these gentiles. The great impasse has been decided and it seems that Paul's idea has won. Everyone now knows the rules, knows the way going forward, and there will be great unity.

This is a wonderful picture of great agreement in the young church, except for one small problem. It seems there was one very strong dissenter from that agreement—my friend Paul. While it may not seem like it in Acts, the question of idol meat will arise once more, only this time it will be in Corinth. Perhaps the issue was not quite as settled as Luke makes it appear.

Blocks of Wood

God of the Whole World

WITH THE JUDGMENT THAT the gentiles would be allowed into the church, Paul increased the pace of his preaching and travels. He traveled throughout Asia Minor and even crossed over into Europe. Often, he did not last very long in the cities he visited. In some places very little was accomplished, while in others, his preaching caused a great deal of commotion, and Paul was forced to leave. Eventually he made his way to Corinth, one of the largest cities in Greece. In many ways Corinth was a crossroads of the Empire, and Paul decided to stay there for eighteen months, from late AD 49 to early 51.

Corinth was a young and vibrant city. It had only been rebuilt a century earlier by Julius Caesar, and it was perhaps the fastest growing city in the Mediterranean. It was located on a narrow isthmus that connected mainland Greece to the Achaia peninsula. The isthmus was only six miles wide, and there was a seaport located on either side of Corinth. Instead of ships traveling all the way around Greece in hope of gaining favorable winds, often those ships would unload their cargo on one side of Corinth, transport those goods overland to the port on the opposite side, and be reloaded onto a different ship there. Not only was this a major shipping and trade hub, but if one wanted to travel from the mainland to the peninsula in Greece, the only way to get there was to go through Corinth.

Yet Corinth was important for other reasons as well. It was the home to over ten pagan temples, representing the worship of Aphrodite, Asklepios, Neptune, Apollo, and Demeter, along with others. This created an accepting atmosphere for religious worship, albeit in a free-for-all kind of way. At the Temple of Demeter, women led the worship in an ecstatic manner. At the temple of Aphrodite, the worship consisted of participation with a temple prostitute. These prostitutes were so common, and the moral life of Corinth so lax that other Greek writers would label prostitutes from other areas of Greece "Corinthian girls." And at the temple of Asklepios people came from all over the empire to seek answers from this god of healing. People would bring an offering for the gods contained in a pottery shaped like the body part which was causing them pain. One can not only imagine all of the varied and interesting shapes these pieces of pottery formed but see the examples that have been found in remains from that period. After giving the offering to the priest, they would wait for the priest to get an answer from the god. Often the wait lasted for days so there was reason to stay in this cosmopolitan, and very diverse city. Since many of these folks travelled from all across the empire, some even needed tents while they waited for the priest to return with the healing words from the pagan god. Paul saw an opportunity here, so he stayed in Corinth as well employing his talents as a tent-maker to support himself.

In AD 49 the emperor Claudius had grown tired of the problems from the Jewish community, and he had expelled all Jews from Rome. Two of the Jews expelled were Priscilla and Acquila. Like so many others of that time, the couple headed to the growing city of Corinth. One of the people they met in Corinth was another newly arrived traveler, my friend Paul. Others listened to Paul's message in Corinth, and the church located there grew while Paul resided in Corinth. After staying in Corinth for eighteen months Paul moved on to preach in other locations, and the church he left behind moved on without Paul.

In Paul's absence, a number of issues arose in the young church. One of the issues was a similar problem to what had happened in Galatia. In Galatia the issues were circumcision and keeping the kosher food laws, but this time it was different. In Galatia the dividing line was very clearly established along Jewish and gentile concerns, but this was not the case here. The issue was simple enough, there were people in the church at Corinth who were eating meat that had been sacrificed to pagan idols. According to Acts 15 the response to this issue should be clear—there was a supposed agreement between the church in Jerusalem, and Paul's faction that Gentiles would be allowed into the church as long as they avoided meat that had been sacrificed to idols. In Paul's absence, people in the church of Corinth were doing this exact thing. Apparently, this action bothered some of the people in the church, and they were among those who had written Paul and asked him to stop the practice within the church. We know this was part of the letter Paul received because he starts chapter 8 by stating, "now about food sacrificed to idols."

It was understandable that not only those in the church, but people all over the Empire would eat this meat. It was simply the economical thing to do. During the pagan feasts animals would be killed in a sacrifice to the gods, and the fat of the animals would be burned during the impressive ceremonies. Then the remaining meat would be sold in the markets. The money from the sale of the meat would go to support the activities in the temple, but it was also the cheapest time of the year for a citizen to buy meat. During the pagan festivals the number of animals being killed meant there was plenty of meat at the market, and the prices for buying meat would tumble. For people who would not often get to enjoy the presence of meat in their diets, this was a benefit. Some of these newer believers would purchase meat at this economical time and would bring it into the church to share in community meals together. This meat represented a problem for some older, Jewish believers in Corinth, and some wanted Paul to speak up, and defend the agreement outlined in Acts 15.

The church awaited Paul's response on this, and a number of other issues. In chapter 8 Paul tackled this problem, and his answer was probably surprising to his first readers, and slightly surprising today. Paul simply refused to prohibit this practice. It is obvious from his words in 1 Corinthians that he does not seem to consider this a dangerous or sinful practice at all. For some of those in Corinth, and perhaps for modern readers of Acts, this revelation might come as a surprise. In response to the question, Paul replied with these words,

> So then, about eating food sacrificed to idols: We know that "An idol is nothing at all in the world" and that "There is no God but one." For even if there are so-called gods, whether in heaven or on earth (as indeed there are many "gods" and many "lords"), yet for us there is but one God, the Father, from whom all things came and for whom we live; and there is but one Lord, Jesus Christ, through whom all things came and through whom we live. (1 Cor 8:4–6, NIV)

This short exchange gives us a clear window into the thinking of Paul, and it is easy to see. Paul's logic is that idols are nothing. They are simply blocks of wood or stone fashioned by human hands. They have no power, no authority and reflect nothing at all. Why would you be bothered that the animal was killed in relation to a block of wood? It means nothing. I am sure that Paul had Psalm 115 in mind as he penned these words to his church in Corinth.

> But their idols are silver and gold,
> made by human hands.
> They have mouths, but cannot speak,
> eyes, but cannot see.
> They have ears, but cannot hear,
> noses, but cannot smell.
> They have hands, but cannot feel,
> feet, but cannot walk,
> nor can they utter a sound with their throats. (Ps 115:4–7, NIV)

Yet I think that Paul goes even further than this. My friend Paul would remind these believers that when anyone gets up in arms over meat that has been sacrificed to idols, it is they who ascribe to the idol power which it does not have. When we get bothered about an idol, the only ones who seem to believe that the idol has any power are the Christians. At best, this sends a mixed message to the larger culture, so Paul gently reminded them that there are more important issues than meat that has been sacrificed to idols.

While this might be surprising to the modern reader, we should not forget the important issue that drives Paul's thinking here. It was the central issue for Paul that drove his thinking on a number of other issues as well. If Christians, through their actions, act as if idols actually have power, then we are undermining the idea of the monotheism of God. For Paul it was central that God was a God of the whole Earth. If these idols have power, then we are saying that God is not God of the whole world, but only for those who believe in the Jewish God. Yet the Hebrew Scriptures do not declare that God is only God of the Jewish tribe, but everyone and everywhere. "Hear O Israel, the Lord our God, the Lord is one." If the idols have power, then God is diminished, and that is a point that Paul is not willing to concede.

It is also a point that we should not concede today, but it is one that we do frequently. A few years ago, my daughter was attending a youth retreat. The well-meaning speaker told the kids that a Christian must avoid "secular" music and should only listen to "Christian" music. My daughter was frustrated somewhat with that message and spent a few weeks trying to process her feelings on the topic. Just a few weeks later she went on a college visit and found herself at a university on the day of a choral concert. Since music was a love for her, she attended the concert. The concert featured a variety of selections. Negro spirituals, Broadway medleys, madrigals, and an eight-part rendition of "A Mighty Fortress" were all featured. At the beginning of the concert the director introduced the evening, and asked the audience to join him in prayer, and I will never forget his prayer. He said, "Lord, we praise you for the gift of music. We thank you because you created every rhythm, every melody, and every harmony. Lord, you created all of it."

Within a few weeks my daughter had been exposed to both sides of the same argument that Corinth experienced. At the youth retreat she heard that some music must be avoided because it was "secular." At the Christian university she heard that God is the creator of all music. As the director prayed, I smiled. I smiled because his words resonated with me. These words resonated because I heard these words from my friend Paul.

Back in Corinth the stronger members of the church there were surprised at Paul's words. They had been believers for quite some time now. They were accustomed to the old, Jewish expectations. They were strong and steadfast in their faith and had expected Paul to say something different in his letter. Yet there was one more surprise in the letter that caused these believers to really examine their position. In 1 Cor. 8:7–12, Paul had called them "weak" in their faith. How could Paul say that about them? They were the ones who knew and followed the rules. They were the ones who took special care to avoid anything that might be a problem. These older believers were disciplined and rigorously avoided certain things. They wanted nothing to do with an idol, and Paul had called them weak. Those words stung.

Yet the issue for Paul was crystal clear. Their Jewish God, the God of Israel, had raised Jesus from the dead. The same power which raised Jesus from the dead was available to the believers in Corinth, and yet they were acting as if the idol made by human hands was somehow threatening the power of Christ in them. Living in that fear was a sign of weakness, and there was no need to be fearful. In Paul's mind, those who lived without that fear are actually stronger, and Paul made this observation known. It might have been a surprise to some in Corinth, but we have to admit, the confidence of Paul was contagious.

There is one other issue that we cannot hide from in Corinth. Paul was never really in agreement with the compromise Luke described in Acts 15. This can make some people upset, but it shouldn't. Luke was trying to describe a new religion to his Roman readers, and he naturally diminished some disagreements within the church. We do the same thing still today. While Paul was happy that the gentiles were going to be accepted in the church, he had deep reservations about conceding what he considered vital. For

Paul, agreeing to any dietary restriction would drain the gospel of its core message, and Paul could not give any ground here.

The message of the gospel was simple, and Paul preached from Genesis 15 in every city he visited—Abraham believed God, and it was counted as righteousness. If you believed that Jesus died and rose again, that faith makes an eternal difference. If anyone adds that faith must also be accompanied by eating certain types of food, then Christianity is no longer defined by the death and resurrection of Jesus, but also by something else. Anything else betrays the central focus of the resurrection. As soon as faith becomes about the necessity of circumcision, or the avoidance of idol meat, then everything has changed, and not for the better. Someone can still be a good person, and be a moral person, but they are no longer a Christian person. The people of Corinth thought the issue was about meat, but Paul knew better. Hopefully, we know better as well.

Failure Times Two
The Dual Role of the Law

THROUGHOUT HIS MINISTRY PAUL continued to fight the same battle that he described in Galatians. We find it easy to forget the culture of Paul's time, and that is unfortunate, because if we forget the history of the New Testament, we will not understand what Paul is trying to say. The early church was overwhelmingly Jewish. In fact, for the first decade or so after the resurrection, the church was entirely Jewish. We mistakenly think that Pentecost was the place where the church became a diverse institution, but Pentecost was a Jewish festival, and those attending would have been only Jews. It is easy to forget this when reading Acts, but the gentiles were not a part of the church until Paul started his ministry somewhere around AD 47.

As a result, the early church easily imported Jewish traditions and expectations into their worship and practice. It is hard for us to remember, but in these early years Christianity was another Jewish sect vying for attention within the larger, diverse Roman Empire. This is why the words of Paul created such an earthquake. While it was possible to convert to Judaism in the first century, it was not a common impulse within Judaism. Paul was unique in that he was actively seeking converts. More importantly Paul was allowing these converts to come into the early church without requiring them to perform the basic, Jewish duties that the law required. These new gentiles found the Jewish regulations not only odd, but they did not see the need to follow the regulations themselves. The existing Jewish believers considered this to be a problem. The tension this created was a constant presence in all of the churches Paul started.

This was a basic religious expectation, but it was also a practical problem as well. It is not hard to understand the argument of these Jewish believers. "If I had to be circumcised, they should have to do this basic thing that I did." Another argument would have been, "I would like to go to Famous Dave's for some good barbecue, but I don't. Therefore, neither should these new believers." Yet this is exactly what Paul is saying. These new additions to the church were being allowed to do things, and eat things that the established believers never did, and it created tension. Paul addressed these objections when he wrote,

> What I mean is this: The law, introduced 430 years later, does not set aside the covenant previously established by God and thus do away with the promise. For if the inheritance depends on the law, then it no longer depends on the promise; but God in his grace gave it to Abraham through a promise. (Gal. 3:17–18)

This sent shock waves through many of the early churches. Paul seemed to be telling people that the law was not needed, and that it was no longer useful. His critics used this claim against Paul like a weapon, and they wanted to wound him with it. The problem was that his critics either did not understand Paul, or were purposefully misrepresenting him, so it forced Paul to explain his position about the law more fully. To be fair we do not understand Paul much better than his critics, even though we have the luxury of hundreds of years of hindsight. Paul's simple point was that the law was not originally a part of God's covenant with his people. God established a relationship with Abraham, and walked through the covenant with him long before the law was given to Moses. If God established his people prior to the presence of the law, then why is it a surprise that he was doing the same thing in Paul's time? Furthermore, if God established this relationship with the Jews in the absence of the law, why would these Jewish believers object to God doing the same thing with the gentiles?

It was at this point of the conversation that his critics pounced. If the law was not present, and if it is so unnecessary, then why was the law even given? Or, Paul, why do you hate the law so much? Paul was on the defensive and his answer was once again surprising. He started by writing this in Gal 3:19, "Why, then, was the law given at all? It was added because of transgressions until the Seed to whom the promise referred had come." Paul's answer was that the law was given not because it was God's original redemptive plan, but in response to our rebellion. It was a needed response to our fall. The purpose of the law here is twofold. First, it has a teaching element. It is meant to tell us exactly what a transgression, or purposeful sin is. It informs us that our actions are not just vaguely wrong, but these actions go against a standard that God expects., and the law explains that standard. The law changes the character of our actions. It changes our behavior from a generalized sense of wrongdoing to a specific violation of a known command of God. We now know we rebel against God, and we know that we need a redemptive action.

Its first role is educational, but the second role the law has is protective. Hopefully, the law would restrain us in anticipation of God's true redemptive purpose—Christ. Paul explains this in Gal 3:23–25:

> Before the coming of this faith, we were held in custody under the law, locked up until the faith that was to come would be revealed. So the law was our guardian until Christ came that we might be justified by faith. Now that this faith has come, we are no longer under a guardian. (NIV)

The word translated as "guardian" here is the Greek word "pedagogue." A pedagogue was a slave who was assigned the task to watch over the children. The slave would protect, teach, and punish the child for wrongdoing. Often the pedagogue would be quite strict with any children under his charge, because it was his job to keep the child safe. This is the role that Paul states the law had. It was there for a time, and the law was to teach, guide, and keep the Jews from being utterly destructive. Yet the pedagogue only ruled over a child for a limited time. It was expected that the child would grow, mature, and eventually care for him or herself. The problem for Paul was not that the law was bad, but that it was useful for only a limited time, and because of Christ, that time had passed.

We read these same passages and see a different issue. In our time the issue of legalism arises with each generation. Therefore, when we read these words about the law, we read the New Testament through the lens we inherited from Martin Luther. The issue, we think, is that Christians are following the rulebook in a vain attempt to earn heavenly points from God. Since the time of Martin Luther, we have tended to read Paul the same way that Luther had, but Luther was dealing with issues from his time, and not the time of Paul. While discouraging legalism may be a worthy goal by itself, that issue is not in Paul's mind at all. Legalism is a modern concern, while Paul had more important things to consider.

When gentile believers willingly seek to express their Christian faith by following the Jewish law, the issue that bothered Paul so much was not legalism. The issue was one of timing and maturity. Any effort to follow the demands of the law was to return to a time and system that was not full, whole, or complete. Paul wrote, "when the fullness of time had come," the Father sent his Son. Returning to the law meant that believers were abandoning this Christ-centered maturity for a time that was marked by a need for a baby-sitter. Adults do not need baby-sitters, children do.

This was the heart of Paul's argument, but it was not received well by those on the other side of the debate. In response Paul went even deeper into his argument, and Israel's past in chapter 4 of Galatians. Paul starts out with a clear statement that seems like a summary of what he has been saying in chapter 3.

> So also, when we were underage, we were in slavery under the elemental spiritual forces of the world. But when the set time had fully come, God sent his Son, born of a woman, born under the law, to redeem those under the law, that we might receive adoption to sonship. Because you are his sons, God sent the Spirit of

his Son into our hearts, the Spirit who calls out, "Abba, Father." So you are no longer a slave, but God's child; and since you are his child, God has made you also an heir. (Gal 4:3–6, NIV)

When we were young, we needed the supervision of the pedagogue to keep us safe, and to properly train us. This is the same way we needed the law. The law was there to train us, inform us, and keep us safe from ourselves. When we mature, we no longer need to pedagogue to watch our every move, and when we reach maturity, we no longer need the law, whose role is only temporary, to do the same thing.

Yet Paul does not stop here, he intensifies his argument in a way the most devoted Jewish believer would have recognized. However, since we are not Jewish, we usually miss the impact of what comes next. The problem is the "Abba, Father" of verse six. Most people read those words, and it throws them off the trail of Paul's thought. Automatically, we are directed to the words of Jesus on the cross in the Gospel of Mark. Once there we become lost about what Paul says next. A simple read through most commentaries on Galatians will reflect this confusion. Later in chapter 4 Paul writes:

Tell me, you who want to be under the law, are you not aware of what the law says? For it is written that Abraham had two sons, one by the slave woman and the other by the free woman. His son by the slave woman was born according to the flesh, but his son by the free woman was born as the result of a divine promise. These things are being taken figuratively: The women represent two covenants. One covenant is from Mount Sinai and bears children who are to be slaves: This is Hagar. Now Hagar stands for Mount Sinai in Arabia and corresponds to the present city of Jerusalem, because she is in slavery with her children. But the Jerusalem that is above is free, and she is our mother.

Paul then further adds:

> Now you, brothers and sisters, like Isaac, are children of promise. At that time the son born according to the flesh persecuted the son born by the power of the Spirit. It is the same now. But what does Scripture say? "Get rid of the slave woman and her son, for the slave woman's son will never share in the inheritance with the free woman's son." Therefore, brothers and sisters, we are not children of the slave woman, but of the free woman. (Gal 4:21–31, NIV)

This is where many people lose Paul. It is easy to do, because Paul often rushes from thought to thought in a cascading series of dense sentences, and in Galatians these thoughts are smashed together in ways that make Paul tough to follow. When most people read the "Abba, Father" of verse 6, they immediately hear the words of Jesus on the cross in Mark 14. How does one go to this discussion of Sarah and Hagar from the words of Jesus on the cross? It is a dilemma where many commentators find themselves.

Yet Paul's argument is not that difficult if one remembers that Paul is a Jew and thought in very Jewish ways. The problem we Christians have is in immediately running to Mark 14 when we read, "Abba Father." While Paul wrote a large portion of our New Testament, it is easy to forget that he was a Jew, and was a child of the Pentateuch, the first five books of the Old Testament. We should remember that Jesus was not the first person in Scripture to utter the word, "Abba." The first person to say this was Isaac. Paul was aware of this, and in Galatians 4 Paul is not thinking about Jesus, but was re-telling the story of Genesis 22, and the sacrifice of Isaac on Mount Moriah. As father and son ascend the mountain in Gen 22:7, Isaac looks over to his father and says, "Abba, Father, where is the lamb?" If we can remember that Paul is referencing Abraham and Isaac, then the rest of his argument here becomes clear.

As soon as Paul begins talking about two sons, we are back into the world of a family squabble. The issue is, who is in the family of God? With the "Abba, Father" of Galatians 4:6 we know Paul's answer. The legitimate child is the child of the promise—the one who said, "Abba, Father," Isaac. Those that seek participation through submitting to the demands of the law as an adult are acting like Ishmael, Isaac's half brother.

We need to remember the contentious issue that was causing the trouble in Galatia. There were people who were convincing the gentiles that in order to become part of God's family, they had to submit to Jewish expectations, and all of the requirements of the law. As a result, the men in Galatia were submitting to the practice of circumcision as a requirement for their participation in the church, and full acceptance into God's family. In Galatians 4 Paul is countering with the argument that the true child of God is not the one who undergoes circumcision, but the one who cries, "Abba, Father" like Isaac. We know that Isaac is the rightful heir, because he was the child promised to Abraham, a promise that came years before the birth of Ishmael, and centuries before the giving of the law.

Even though God promised a son to Abraham and his wife, Sarah, they grew tired of waiting, and they took matters into their own hands. As a result, a son, named Ishmael, was born to Abraham through Sarah's servant, Hagar. Yet this child was not the son that God promised to them. After years of frustration, jealousy and estrangement, Sarah finally gives birth to a son named Isaac, the child of the promise. It is at this point that the covenant of circumcision is introduced. Both sons, Isaac and Ishmael, undergo this religious procedure at the same time. Yet when this happens Isaac is a baby, but Ishmael is already thirteen years old.

When one is Jewish the age of thirteen is deeply meaningful. Every Jewish boy participates in his Bar Mitzvah at age thirteen. This is more than a cute ceremony but is considered the time when a Jewish boy becomes a man, and responsible for the covenant and the commandments. Naturally when a Jew looks back on this story, it is only Isaac who is circumcised as a child, while Ishmael is clearly an adult when he is circumcised.

We have finally arrived at the heart of Paul's argument here. When the Galatians decide to undergo circumcision as an adult, they are not doing anything that would make them more favored by God. After all, the Jews trace their lineage back through the promised son Isaac, not through Ishmael, who was the child of a slave. If you are circumcised as an adult, you are not acting like Isaac at all, but are actually doing the exact same thing as Ishmael. They are submitting to the very thing that will actually mark them as a slave for life. Paul is writing that these Jewish believers are not only mistaken about the status of these new gentiles, they are confused about their own Jewish heritage and are giving the gentiles terrible advice. The slave is the one who submits to circumcision, the child is the one who is part of the promise, and the promise came before either the law, or the practice of circumcision. The child of the promise is the one who is enabled to say, "Abba, Father."

The argument has now come full circle. There were those who told these gentile believers that they were not really a full part of God's family unless they were circumcised and followed all of the Jewish requirements. If they wanted to share in their full rights as God's family, they needed to show the full marks of that inheritance. Paul simply goes back to the Jewish story and shows them that if circumcision was the full expression of who was God's family, then Ishmael would be the child of God since Ishmael did the exact same thing that these Galatians were being asked to do. Any attempt to make adherence to the law or the practice of circumcision the centerpiece of joining God's family would be a failure. This failure was not because Paul was changing the expectations, but because God established his people and family before either the law came to Israel. God's expectations are simple—believe and obey, just like Abraham and Isaac. The law was only a later addition to help a rebellious people. It never was the full expression of God's design. The people who descended from the son who said "Abba, Father" should know this. A person with impeccable Jewish credentials could hopefully convince these new believers of this. My friend Paul tried to remind them.

Paul would say the same thing today. In each generation believers try to demonstrate their faith through effort. The issue is not that we are attempting to earn a certain status before God, but we start to see that if other people are in the family, they must look like us, and think like us. Our inclusion into God's family started and finished with the death and resurrection of Jesus. God's family does not look like me but is comprised of all those who find their identity in Christ. Paul is still reminding us.

Group Failure
The Sin of Humanity

We are so fortunate to have all of these letters from the hand of Paul still with us. It is not hard to imagine Paul sitting down and writing these words directly to us. Many believers are inspired by this thought, yet it is vital to remember that Paul was not writing to us, but to a particular group of people, and was addressing a specific situation. Two thousand years later we read these words, and since we are unaware of the situation, it is easy to take the wrong lesson from what Paul has written. The words in the New Testament represent one side of an ongoing conversation, and this is particularly true with Paul's letters. We do the best we can to reconstruct the other half of the conversation, but this can be difficult. There is danger in getting this wrong. If we do not do it correctly, we can take a meaning from Paul that he never intended. Since we do not have the other half of the conversation, it is easy to jump to hasty conclusions and make this mistake. We do not do it on purpose, but we just assume that Paul is addressing our modern problem or operates from the same set of assumptions that we do. This is simply not the case, and one of our problem areas is Romans 7.

There is often a debate around Paul's words in Romans 7. The debate rages around whom Paul is addressing in this chapter. On one side stand those who argue that Paul is describing the difference between a pre-Christian and a post-Christian life. Others argue for a more nuanced position. They hold that Paul is talking about two different developments in the Christian life but is contrasting life as a Christian before the presence of the Holy Spirit, and a more triumphant life after the arrival of the personal acceptance of the Holy Spirit. While this debate continues to rage, it should be noted that both of these conclusions approach the passage from an individualistic perspective. This is not surprising since we come to the text from the shared background of the individualistic West. While this is natural for us, this was not the background of my friend Paul, and he would have found such an approach odd, and not his meaning at all.

Paul was a person very firmly rooted in his historical context. In his case, it is a decidedly Jewish context. Sometimes we like to remove the Bible from its context in an effort to make it speak to us more effectively, but that is a dangerous practice. Once we remove the Bible from its history, we can make it say something it never intended to say. Once removed from its history, we can make the Bible say whatever we want it to say. As a result, all we have done is weaken the timeless message of Scripture, just to make it say something we want it to say now. This was not Paul's concern, and it wasn't his concern in Romans 7.

We should not forget what is at stake here. Paul is writing to a church divided along the familiar Jew/Gentile divide. This was particularly true in Rome, although for different reasons than what we saw earlier in Galatia. The Jews had been forced to leave Rome by the emperor Claudius in AD 49, only to be allowed back in 54. To the Jewish believers returning to Rome, they would find their church completely gentile in composition. With the return of the Jewish believers, one might expect familiar fault lines to develop in the church, and Paul is addressing this church with the hopes of avoiding the rifts he had witnessed in other places. In fact, one simply cannot appreciate Romans without being aware of this dividing line between Jew and Gentile. Paul was not writing as an individual Christian addressing individual concerns. Instead, Paul wrote in a collectivist time, and wrote to people who saw the world through the eyes of their group identity.

Romans 1 starts with a natural reminder that the gentiles were people well acquainted with sin. The pagan world was so corrupt that their idolatry has led to a number of sinful practices. Naturally, the Jewish believers would have enthusiastically agreed with this assessment, so Paul tells them in chapter 2 that they are no better, and do not possess an "inside track" to God. This results in Paul's great declaration in chapter 3, that all have sinned and have fallen short of the glory of God. The unexpected surprise of Paul's argument happens in chapter 4 where Paul returns to Abraham to demonstrate his point. One might expect the Jews to be relieved that Paul uses Abraham to further his point, but Paul gives his familiar reply that Abraham is our example, but not because of the law, but because he simply believed God—he had faith.

The modern reader usually does not notice the impact of what Paul has just stated. Purposefully he has just left the importance of the law out of his argument. The Jewish believers would have immediately noticed this and asked, "what about the law?" The law was the pinnacle of the Jewish people, and they would have wondered what role Paul envisioned for the law. Paul's answer to this question is what we read in chapters 5–7. In chapter 5 Paul gives the law an educational function, which we will explore in the next chapter of this book. The argument is expanded in chapter 6, where Paul reminds the Jewish believers that they should not be slaves to sin. This is loaded language geared directly for the Jewish believers. The Jews would never consider themselves slaves, they were offspring of the promised son, Isaac. Jewish believers would also respond by pointing to the law. "We are not slaves to sin, we not only possess the law, but we know the law. The law protects us from ever being slaves to sin." Paul is now compelled to either defend the law, or to find a place for the law for these Jewish believers that still demonstrates their need for Christ. This leads us to our present discussion of Romans 7 and our tendency to read this in an individualistic manner.

We need to remember the flow of Paul's argument in this letter. Paul is not writing to scattered individuals, but to the church in Rome, which is divided along these ethnic lines. Paul is specifically writing to the Jewish believers here, and finding a place for their beloved law, after diminishing it in his opening chapters.

The modern reader usually becomes distracted by the first-person writing style that was employed through most of chapter 7. "I would not have even known what it means to covet without the law." We read this and assume that Paul is talking about himself, but we miss two big pieces of evidence here in verses 7 and 14. Paul begins these larger sections with the first-person plural construction. "What shall we say then?" Perhaps we have missed the obvious. Paul wrote this section with his own people in mind—believers from a Jewish background. Paul even explicitly tells us what he is doing in the first verse of Romans 7, when he writes, "I am speaking to those who know the law."

This should not surprise us. When one continues to read Romans, Paul explicitly announces he has Israel in mind in chapters 9—11. This is not a new topic, but a continuation of what has been in Paul's mind all along. Having already announced that the law's purpose was educational, Paul tells everyone exactly how that role is experienced in real life. Since the Jews are the people who have possessed the law, he needs to explain this as a representative of the Jewish people. To Jews, the law was the highest expression of God for humanity, and this attitude was still prominent with the Jewish believers in the church. In Galatia, this attitude had already caused a divide in which Paul seemed to be on the losing side. Now that the Jews had rejoined the church in Rome, Paul wants to prevent a similar problem in the capital of the Empire.

Once again, the focus of this entire argument is not what makes Paul struggle, but does the law have any value for believers? Paul's answer is simple, and he speaks on behalf of the people who have valued the law. Yes, the law has always been important. The law has a teaching role. I would not have even known what sin was if it had not been for the law telling me. Then a surprising thing happened, at least to those who valued the law so much. Paul tells them that the law actually worked against them. When the law told the Jews what sin was, it did not produce a revulsion against sin. Instead, it created a desire to do the very thing that they knew to be wrong. This is not solely Paul's problem. This is the problem of everyone who knows the law. How many of us have seen the twisted look on the face of an angelic two-year old, who after being told not to do something, becomes obsessed with doing that very thing? This is what the law does. It does not bring life to those who try to follow it. It actually creates a desire to do what has been labeled as wrong. The law actually produces death in us.

This point would have angered those who were proud of their Jewish heritage. They would have been astounded at Paul's negativity towards the law. Their complaint would have been, "Paul why do you think the law is so bad? God gave the law to us." Paul's short response is found in verse 12, "So then, the law is holy, and the commandment is holy, righteous and good." This short reply at first confused those with a Jewish background. How could Paul say that the law brings death, while at the same time say it is holy and good? The answer to this question gets to the heart of what my friend Paul thought about the law.

The heart of the issue for Paul was the purpose of the law. For the most part his Jewish brethren all thought the law was the paramount expression of God's will for his people, and the force that brought life and set them apart. After his experience on the Damascus Road, Paul thought differently. If the law was meant to bring life, then why has Israel struggled so much with it? If it was intended to bring life, then why has the presence of the law left us alienated from the rest of the world? If the law was meant to bring life, why do we still struggle so much with even the most basic expression of the law? Perhaps the purpose of the law has been misunderstood. Maybe it was never intended to bring life. Yes, God gave the law to the Jews, but maybe the purpose of the law was not what many of the Jews thought. This is where Paul departed from his contemporaries, and our individualistic readings of Romans miss this.

This is where the next task of the law enters our picture. We have already admitted that the law identifies sin, and educates about its dangers, but it also serves to intensify our experience of sin. This seems counter-intuitive yet again. How does the law intensify sin? Paul states this plainly, although many have refused to see this aspect of the law. In verse 13 Paul states, "so that through the commandment sin might become utterly sinful." This is the part of the argument that is difficult to comprehend. Everyone is aware that there is wrong in the world, and we live in this world where sin is so much in evidence. Yet Paul states the purpose of the law is to identify sin as contrary to God and force us to go against God when we do it. In essence, because of the law, our wrongdoing is turned into purposeful rebellion against God. Because the law tells us about the nature of sin, we become aware, we become deliberate, and we become purposeful when we sin. The law changes the character of the wrong that we do.

This is not the weight that Paul alone was bearing, but it was the weight that all of Israel was called to bear. The problem was that this weight had broken Israel. Although they knew the route they were to take, Israel had again and again fallen back to rebellion and idol worship. In the midst of this Israel still knew the things they were not to do, but this knowledge had separated them from all other nations. Just knowing the wrong was not enough, and Israel lived with this desperate, futile attempt to merely avoid sin. Somehow more was needed.

Triumphantly, this is where Jesus enters Paul's argument. At the end of chapter 7 Paul leaves the reader in an utterly hopeless place. "What a wretched man I am! Who will rescue me from this body that is subject to death?" Once again, we are tempted to read this as a window into Paul's personal struggle, but that would miss the larger argument. Paul, writing for the Jewish people, stated that all who seek to live according to the law find themselves subject to death. This is the natural result of the law. The great celebratory note opens chapter 8. "Therefore, there is now no condemnation for those who are in Christ Jesus." If Paul was speaking only about his own struggle, we should expect to find "there is no condemnation for me." Yet Paul is speaking about everyone who seeks to live according to the law. There is no condemnation for the plural those are in Christ. This is further shown in verse 2 when Paul states that Christ has set "you" free. If Paul is speaking about himself, we should expect to find the singular "me."

Why is this important? We tend to read this section and minimize Paul's argument to a discussion about the relative usefulness of legalistic living. An individualistic reading of Paul here leads naturally to this conclusion. Yet there is much more at stake for Paul. When we turn this passage into Paul writing about a personal struggle with legalism, we ignore some very dire language Paul uses about "death," and Paul is a Christian either way. He either becomes a Christian struggling with legalism, or a Christian freed from it. This is clearly not Paul's intent. The law is inadequate and has no place in the Christian life because it leads to death. One can attempt to fulfill the law, but the problem is not that it cannot be done, the problem is that even if one does it, it leads inevitably to death. Any pursuit of the law as a goal leads directly away from Christ. It is possible to keep the law and Paul admits this possibility in Philippians 3, but even if it is kept perfectly, it does not lead anyone closer to God.

The reason it leads away is because the law was never intended to make people good. The purpose of the law was to tell us that the wrong we do is actually sin and make us responsible for it. Therefore, when we try to collectively follow the law, the group is frustrated because instead of finding life, we find ourselves condemned. We try to be good, but the law just tells us that we have failed and fallen short. That is why we are wretched. It would take the death of Israel's true representative to undo the damage that the law has done.

Suddenly a group of Jews arose that claimed a man named Jesus was that representative. A Roman cross would have disqualified Jesus from being seen as that representative, but these people were making strange claims about a resurrection. Paul was sent to investigate these believers and discipline them accordingly. Then this Jesus somehow talked to him on that road to Damascus. This Jesus was alive and that changed everything. That is why there is no condemnation for those in Christ, and the benefit of what Christ has done flowed to more people than just my friend Paul. It also flowed to gentiles.

Personal Failure

My Sin

It may seem odd after talking about how Paul geared his comments in chapter 7 to the Jews, but Paul does talk about how the individual experiences sin. This is a topic that was prominent in ancient times, and it is still a topic that generates discussion in modern times as well.

Paul actually had a great deal to say on the topic of sin, but somehow, we have missed the importance of the things he said. We still struggle with this topic today, and so we are not very different from those within the church of Rome. If one listens to the debate within the church today, one can hear the debate breaking down along lines that Paul would have found odd. On one side we find a wing of Christianity that proclaims sin is an unavoidable part of everyday life. Sin is not only there, but it is something we do every single day in thought, word and deed. One other significant tradition of Christianity also struggles with this topic, as we use inexact words in a manner that often leaves our people confused about the extent of sin, and the extent of our redemption. Thankfully, Paul was much more exact in his language than we are with ours when he wrote chapter 5 of Romans.

I think we need to remember the question that Paul was seeking to answer in this section. He had just declared that all have sinned and have fallen short of the glory of God in chapter 3. Then in chapter 4 Paul had just declared that righteousness did not come through the law. The next inevitable question for Jewish believers would have been—then why was the law even given? Certainly, God gave the law for a reason. In chapter 5 Paul tells the reader with clarity why the law was given, and he does so in a manner that informs the individual. Paul begins chapter 5 by once again declaring that we were ungodly. The good news for all of us is that even though we were sinners, Christ died for us. Because of this death we can now be reconciled to God. Yet the question for Jewish believers still hung in the air—what purpose does the law serve?

Paul started in verse 12 by telling the readers that we know sin is a reality, because there is the reality of death all around us. Paul then argued that death is the result of sin, and we face death because all of us have sinned. This is not the place to start a detailed discussion about Augustinian notions of original sin, and physical vs. environmental transmission. There is certainly a place for a discussion on how we experience sin, but that is not Paul's argument here. Paul made a more general observation. His simple statement was that the presence of death is evidence of the presence of sin.

Paul's argument is relatively straightforward as he begins this section. He simply observes that we know that sin is active because if we look around, we will notice that death is active. The presence of sin and death was a problem, and it was a problem long before the presence of the law. Paul's argument was that the law was given in response to the reality of sin. A Jew would have expected the argument that the law was given to defeat the power of sin, but that is not the argument that Paul made. To anyone with a Jewish background, Paul's next statement is provocative, and completely unexpected. He stated that "sin is not charged to anyone's account where there is no law" (5:13). This is not the victorious statement that Jewish believers would have expected.

This is the same argument he will later make in chapter 7 on a larger scale, but here in chapter 5 the argument is intensely personal. Paul stated that the law educates us about what constitutes sin, and the law somehow intensifies it. Yes, Paul has already made the admission that sin is present, but with the presence of the law sin takes on a different character and we become personally responsible for it. As a result, the presence of the law has this completely unexpected effect, at least for the Jew. Jews want to celebrate the law for its inherent goodness, while Paul stated that when we know the law it has the immediate effect of intensifying our experience with sin. In other words, it makes us aware of its deadly effects. The law brings death to us. This is why Paul cried out at the end of chapter 7, "Who will save me from this body of death?"

There are also some important distinctions here in chapter 5 that most readers of Romans will miss. When we normally talk about sin, we do so by using this one word to describe all ungodly behavior. We simply say "sin." Paul's language is far more varied than our own, and Paul had a number of words for sin at his disposal, and he used a number of these words in chapter 5. Yet these synonyms for sin have some important distinctions, and we miss Paul's argument because these distinctions are often not known.

We do similar things with other words. In my freshman year of college, my roommate was a young man from the south. When December came the first winter snows started to hit our Midwestern campus. The first time it snowed was one of those days when the wind was coming off Lake Michigan and snow was blowing around in the air like a snow globe. To those of us who were from the Midwest, this was a non-event. It could snow like that all day, and nothing would happen. Yet to my southern roommate this was a big event. He came bursting in our dorm room and excitedly said, "Look, it's snowing!" I looked out the window and said, "No, it's not." Frustrated, he looked at the window and said, "Do you not see the snowflakes coming down?" I said, "of course, but that is not snow, it's just blowin' around."

If you had spent your life living in the south, it was plainly snowing outside. Yet, if you grew up in Michigan or northern Ohio, you would be familiar with snow, and what was happening outside was not snow. It was flurries, or just a snow shower blowing through. It was certainly nothing worthy of notice. If one lives in the shadow of the Great Lakes, there are many different words for winter weather.

Paul does the same thing in Romans 5, and he used many words for sin in a similar manner. The first word he used is the well-known word *hamartia*. In Greek *hamartia* simply means anything that misses the mark. Anything which deviates from the intended aim is *hamartia*. Unfortunately, this is where most Christians' understanding of sin begins and ends. If we solely carry this definition to our discussion of sin, it will eventually lead to a theological dead end. It is a dead end that most of us know quite well. If sin is solely described as *hamartia*, then we really do sin every day in word, thought, and deed.

The next word that Paul uses is the less common *paraptoma*, which means a willful misstep. It is not just wandering across a boundary line but knowing that the boundary exists and stepping across that line anyway. Paul did not just stop here, for he used a third word to describe sin, and that word is *parabasis*, which simply means deliberate rebellion. This takes sin to an even deeper, and more purposeful level than *paraptoma*. When the modern reader looks at Romans 5 it is vital to keep the meaning of these words in mind. Without them, we can seriously misunderstand the argument of Paul. This would be a misunderstanding that results in consequences for a modern believer.

Paul freely admitted here, and earlier in chapter 3, that everyone has sinned (*hamartia*), and as a result death is a reality in our world. Yet Paul found it important to ground a certain responsibility in the original sin of Adam. Notice that Paul does not tell us that the problem was the *hamartia*, or general wrongdoing of Adam, but the *parabasis*, or rebellion of Adam. Adam's sin had a unique character that made it affect the whole world, and that was his knowledge of God's expectation. That knowledge changed his wrongdoing into an act that goes against God's character. The phrase is straightforward in the original language and is translated well in the NRSV. "Yet death exercised dominion from Adam to Moses, even over those whose sins were not like the 'rebellious' transgression (*parabasis*) of Adam" (5:14).

Because of this rebellion all of humanity was affected. We now live in a world dominated by sin and death. Some may want to place all the blame on Adam, but Paul has already avoided that argument, as he stated plainly in chapter 3 that everyone has sinned. It is at this point Paul introduced the argument he will make more fully in chapter 7, by introducing it on a smaller scale in chapter 5. Why was the law given? His answer was that it was given to change the character of the wrong we do.

In verse 20 Paul wrote that when the law arrived the result was that sin became utterly sinful. Again, perhaps the NRSV renders it best, "the law came in, with the result that the trespass multiplied" (5:20). This phrase strikes many readers as odd. How can the law actually produce more sin? Yet this is not what Paul is arguing here. The law does not produce sin, but it identifies it. The presence of the law changes *hamartia* into *paraptoma* (willful acts). It is *paraptoma* which is being increased, the willful misstep, not just generalized wrongdoing. Since the presence of the law turns our general wrongdoing into a willful act, the sin now becomes utterly personal and our moral responsibility. Paul explicitly states this in Romans 5:13, "sin is not charged against anyone's account where there is no law." (NIV)

This is the heart of the issue for Paul. For most of his life, Paul had pursued the law as the highest good in the world. Yet even as he pursued the law, he realized that it did not produce the good in him that he had expected. Instead, the law had only intensified sin into willful disobedience, making humanity liable. The Jewish believers were making the exact same mistake as he had. They were tempted to do all of the demands of the law in the hope it would make them alive, but instead they only found an awareness of sin, and a new liability.

This leads us to an inevitable conclusion that impacts our understanding today. All of us live in an imperfect world—a world where *hamartia* is present every day. Even the best of us still struggle with the *hamartia* around us. Some of this is of our own doing, while at other times it is the result of those around us. We speak about sin in such personal terms we often neglect the communal impact of sin. Paul does not. When a drunk driver gets behind the wheel and strikes another car, we are affected by sin.

When a company pollutes the drinking water of a community and people end up sick, we are again in the grip of sin. When government and banks collude with the result being a financial crash, sin is once again throwing its weight around. Sometimes, we struggle with our imperfections. Often our weaknesses and imperfections cause us to feel guilt, and we wonder if God still loves us, since we still struggle with the same issue that has dogged us through the years. Therefore, we are left with frustration, and a sense that we are somehow outside of God's favor.

Yet Paul's words in Romans 5 bring us a note of clarity. While we are impacted by *hamartia* every day, and struggle with our own *hamartia*, this general wrongdoing is not what we are responsible for before God. We are liable for the *paraptoma*, the willful sins, that we do. The purpose of the law is to take our *hamartia*, or failures, and turn it into deliberate acts of rebellion. The role of the law is now made clear, it identifies, and concentrates sin. Only after sin has been identified by the law can it now be dealt with by those who seek to walk with God.

This impacts how we live today. All of us deal with *hamartia*, or our own failures and imperfections. There is no way to avoid these because our world is a living, breathing example of *hamartia* piled thick. Paul declares that while the reality of hamartia is present, we are not guilty of these. In fact, we have no way of knowing what these even are. This is where the law finds its greatest role. The law teaches us what the right is, and what expectations God has for us. Once we know the righteous choice purposefully going against that choice turns *hamartia* into *paraptoma*, or deliberate steps. Paul tells us that this is where we become accountable. We are guilty for what we know and fail to do. Without knowledge of the right, there is no guilt.

Some might again suggest that perhaps it is best that we never spread the good news, because why would we tell people about the right, since it will serve to change their generalized wrong into *paraptoma*. We do so because it is a necessary step to deal with it. We go to the doctor when we have the general sense that we are not feeling well, only to hear the doctor tell us specifically what is wrong. Some people deliberately avoid the doctor for this reason. They do not want to hear the doctor tell them anything is wrong. The problem is that until that wrong is identified, treatment is not possible. The role of the law is to identify the problem, but Jewish believers were treating the law as the remedy for all of the wrong in the world. It was not the remedy, and my friend Paul was trying to let people know.

Nothing New Here

Who Is Special?

PAUL TRAVELLED THROUGHOUT THE eastern portion of the Roman Empire and experienced varying levels of success. As active as Paul was in his travels, he yearned to experience Rome and spread the message of the gospel in the largest city and central gathering place of the empire. With the possible exception of Ephesians, Paul had personal knowledge of all the churches to whom he wrote, and he knew many of the people in those churches. When Paul wrote his letters, he was not engaged in a dry exercise but was writing to people he knew and with whom he shared a personal bond. This was not the case with the church in Rome. As Paul looked to the west and imagined a trip to the capital of the empire, he thought that he should write a letter of introduction and introduce his message to this influential community.

In the mid-50s the timing was perfect for such a letter. In 49 the Emperor Claudius had evicted all the Jews from Rome. With the stroke of the emperor's pen the church in Rome suddenly became entirely gentile in an instant. This made the church in Rome different from the other churches in the Empire where Jewish believers were a part of the church. The expulsion turned out to be short-lived and the Jews were allowed to return in 54 after the death of Claudius. After five years of an entirely gentile church in Rome, the former Jewish believers returned and attempted to re-integrate back into the life of the church. With all of his contacts the word of this change had reached Paul's ears as well. Since relations between Jews and Gentiles were often the problem in Paul's other churches, he thought a well-timed letter might help to stop this common problem from happening in Rome. Paul's letter addressed a host of issues that expressed Christian belief and practice but Paul spent considerable time talking about how Jews and Gentiles can co-exist and thrive in the church.

The potential issue in the church in Rome was a little different than what had plagued many of the other young churches. In the other churches, like the Galatian church, the issue had been under what circumstances would the Gentiles be allowed to participate. The backbone of these churches were the early Jewish believers and Paul had to convince these believers to fully integrate the newer Gentiles into the church. This was definitely not the issue in Rome, but this did not make the potential way forward any easier. In the Roman church the Gentiles had learned to do things without the presence of the earlier Jewish believers. With the recent return of the Jews this church would once again feature both groups worshiping together. Adding to the potential difficulty is that both groups could credibly claim priority over the other group within the life of the church. The dynamics might be potentially explosive.

My friend Paul saw the potential and thought that if the church in Rome splintered along these familiar lines, then the witness of the church would be severely damaged in the place where that damage would be the costliest. The young church could not afford damaging trouble in the capital of the Empire. Paul took his time, considered his words carefully, and wrote his most thoughtful and detailed letter to the church in Rome. Paul wanted to introduce himself to this important church, but it was paramount that both groups considered Jew and Gentile full partners in the kingdom.

I think Paul would be genuinely surprised to discover how some people read Romans 9–11 today. Many find that Paul is endorsing a relatively modern view where God has created a select group on which he focuses his redemptive work called the elect. This is perhaps understandable if we think that Paul's letter is generally addressed to anyone at any particular time. Yet this is not true of any biblical book and can only be true if we forget that every New Testament book was written to a specific situation on the ground at the time of writing. Forgetting this basic fact would be extremely unfortunate in Romans as both Jews and Gentiles are explicitly referenced. When we read Paul's words in the demographic context of the mid 50s, his meaning becomes clear.

In Romans 9–11 Paul is arguing that there is a select group that God has chosen above others. This is correct, but the modern reader's identification of that select group is unnecessarily complicated even though Paul identifies who the select group is—the Jews. This group was granted many advantages over any other group. To the Jews were given the promise, the law, and the Messiah came from their family. What a great history! In fact, everything about this faith flowed from a thoroughly Jewish foundation. Israel's God and Israel's Messiah were the Lord and Savior of the fledgling Christian church as well. In chapter 11 Paul takes great care to remind his readers that the faith to which these Gentiles belonged had secure, Jewish roots. As the Jewish believers returned to the church they helped start, Paul was reminding the gentiles that they should respect and honor the history of these Jewish pioneers. Paul expresses this clearly in Rom 11:17–21:

> If some of the branches have been broken off, and you, though a wild olive shoot, have been grafted in among the others and now share in the nourishing sap from the olive root, do not consider yourself to be superior to those other branches. If you do, consider this: You do not support the root, but the root supports you. You will say then, "Branches were broken off so that I could be grafted in." Granted. But they were broken off because of unbelief, and you stand by faith. Do not be arrogant, but tremble. For if God did not spare the natural branches, he will not spare you either. (NIV)

The heart-rending issue for Paul is that so many of his people had rejected Jesus, who Paul had discovered was the Messiah. We should, of course, remember that this rejection was not universal. Paul, and these returning Jewish believers were a constant reminder that many Jews believed. Here was the first part of the paradox that Paul was navigating in Romans. The Jews, who were the chosen people, were largely rejecting Jesus. Their authentic status as chosen people had not given them any special access or automatic entry into the church.

Then Paul addressed the Gentiles who comprised the majority of the church in Rome. These gentiles were definitely not the chosen people. They were not given the prophets or the law yet somehow were a part of this new church. This is explicitly stated in Rom 9:22–26:

> What if God, although choosing to show his wrath and make his power known, bore with great patience the objects of his wrath—prepared for destruction? What if he did this to make the riches of his glory known to the objects of his mercy, whom he prepared in advance for glory—even us, whom he also called, not only from the Jews but also from the gentiles? As he says in Hosea:
> "I will call them 'my people' who are not my people; and I will call her 'my loved one' who is not my loved one."(NIV)

This is an oddly matched pair for Paul. The chosen Jews are rejecting Christ, while those that are not chosen are eagerly flowing into the church. What is one to make of this unexpected turn of events? One certainly cannot find any shred of the modern argument where there is a group that is foreordained for inclusion. This is the opposite of what we find in Romans where the ones who are largely included were definitely not in the "chosen" group of people.

Later in his life Paul made the same point in a letter he wrote to be passed around from church to church. During his final years as Paul awaited trial, he heard about new churches started by other people. Thrilled with this good news, Paul wanted to write a letter to these people that he did not know. He hoped this letter would be copied, and then sent along to the next church. This is the letter we know as Ephesians, and chapter 1 discusses this idea of who the chosen people are.

> For he chose us in him before the creation of the world to be holy and blameless in his sight. In love he predestined us for adoption to sonship through Jesus Christ, in accordance with his pleasure and will— to the praise of his glorious grace, which he has freely given us in the One he loves. In him we have redemption through his blood, the forgiveness of sins, in accordance with the riches of God's grace that he lavished on us. With all wisdom and understanding, he made known to us the mystery of his will according to his good pleasure, which he purposed in Christ, to be put into effect when the times reach their fulfillment—to bring unity to all things in heaven and on earth under Christ.
>
> In him we were also chosen, having been predestined according to the plan of him who works out everything in conformity with the purpose of his will, in order that we, who were the first to put our hope in Christ, might be for the praise of his glory. And you also were included in Christ when you heard the message of truth, the gospel of your salvation. When you believed, you were marked in him with a seal, the promised Holy Spirit, who is a deposit guaranteeing our inheritance until the redemption of those who are God's possession—to the praise of his glory. (Eph 1:4–14, NIV)

We miss Paul's intent here, even though it is hiding in plain sight. We read Ephesians 1 and when the word "predestined" in verses 5 and 11 is seen we immediately jump to our theories and arguments that arose in the 1500s. Yet these were not the concerns of my friend Paul, and we forget about his times. We read the word "predestined" and forget about everything else in Ephesians 1. In this opening chapter of the letter Paul references two different groups—the "we/us" group, and the "you" group. If we are confused about the identity of these groups, Paul tells us who he is referencing in verse 12. Paul clearly states the "we" group are the first to hope in Christ, which were the Jewish believers. The gentiles would not follow for fifteen to twenty years. We should notice that when Paul talks about being "predestined," it is always in reference to the Jews.

When Paul gets to verse 13, he immediately assures the Gentiles that "you also were included." This is very clear when we remember what Paul was facing. The Jews did have a role to play. They were to bless all nations, and to be the people through whom Christ would come. Even though the Jews had this special calling, the gentiles were now "also included." Here in Ephesians, just as in Romans, there is no distinction between how the chosen group and non-chosen group were being included into God's family. Any modern attempt to find a restricted group with divine benefits forgets the situation and history of my friend Paul.

One cannot find any shred of the modern argument of predestination in Paul. If the chosen group—the elect—can find themselves largely on the outside of the church, while the non-chosen are definitely included, then what possible purpose would any "chosen" group have today? Yet that was the exact condition that sparked Paul's words. The Jews who were chosen to bless the entire world were not believing in Christ, while all the Gentiles were believing. Any time we read Romans 9–11 we must keep this in mind.

I think Paul would be surprised at how much misunderstanding there is of his argument in these chapters. In chapter 9 of Romans Paul wrote these famous words:

> Not only that, but Rebekah's children were conceived at the same time by our father Isaac. Yet, before the twins were born or had done anything good or bad—in order that God's purpose in election might stand: not by works but by him who calls—she was told, "The older will serve the younger." Just as it is written: "Jacob I loved, but Esau I hated." What then shall we say? Is God unjust? Not at all! For he says to Moses, "I will have mercy on whom I have mercy, and I will have compassion on whom I have compassion." (Rom 9:10–15, NIV)

Many modern readers of Romans seem to lift this discussion of Jacob and Esau away from what Paul is personally experiencing in the first century. Without its context this passage becomes a simple statement that God favored one brother over another for reasons that only God knows. His election then, is a mysterious reality and we just need to acknowledge that God will do what God wants and we have no idea why God chooses some over others.

If we apply this text to Paul's situation, a far more satisfactory meaning emerges—a meaning that Paul would have recognized easily. Paul is making a rabbinic argument here in Romans 9 that any Jew would have understood. The argument is that Jews should not be surprised or upset that the Gentiles are now a part of God's family, because this is something that God has done before. By all rights and expectations Esau should have been the son that received the birthright, but it went to Jacob instead. The Jews traced their lineage back through Jacob and considered him one of their great patriarchs of Jewish identity. If the Jews themselves were the beneficiaries of God acting outside of the expected order, then why should they be surprised now if God does this again? The Jews' special status as God's people could be traced to God acting outside of the expected order. If the Jewish believers reacted against God doing something similar now, they were actually questioning their own history.

All of Paul's work in Romans 9–11 seeks to promote mutual understanding and respect between Jews and Gentiles. If the church is going to impact the Roman Empire, the church located in its capitol must be united and demonstrate love in action, even between groups that have little in common. Therefore, the gentiles must respect the Jewish believers. First, their people had carried a relationship with God for centuries and the gentile Savior was part of their people. Secondly, the Jewish believers were the first who had believed in Christ and had brought it to the Gentiles, even if begrudgingly at times. The Jews, on the other hand, must realize that their special relationship with God did not arise from their own talent or choice but the gracious action of God. If God chooses to extend the same gracious initiative to the gentiles, then their response should be welcoming.

What is clear is that in Romans 9–11 Paul is pleased that the non-chosen people are responding to the gospel. Paul's former life had been dedicated to the elevation of his people, the Jews. After the Damascus Road, Paul's entire life was dedicated to reaching these gentiles. At the same time his heart was breaking for his people, the Jews. He yearned for their response to the gospel. Even if it seemed they were denying Jesus now, Paul always left room for their full inclusion later. Paul clearly believed in a group of people chosen by God, but only to serve the larger purpose of belief for everyone. This is what so many miss today. My friend Paul never did.

The Perfect Life
Keeping Every Rule

LIKE MANY PEOPLE I grew up in a church that was well aware of the capacity for humanity to do wrong. We sang hymns with the lyrics, "Would he devote that sacred head for such a worm as I?" It seemed we were well aware of our own sin, and well aware of human failure. We were told weekly in sermons that the problem with humanity was that we are unable to keep the demands of the law. Try as we might, we always fall short. That is our plight—in spite of all of our best efforts, we cannot uphold all of the law. Because we fail at our attempt to keep the law, we need the grace and mercy of Jesus Christ. This has been said so often it has become part of our accepted lexicon. Paul would be puzzled by such a claim.

There are two problems with this often-expressed view. The first is that it turns Christianity into a performance-based exercise. The goal of life is that we are to do good, and this good is expressed in the Jewish law. This is not what we mean, but we follow up this thought with the expression that we are unable to keep the law. We fail doing those things the law requires, and because of that failure we need Jesus Christ. Yet if our problem is an inability to perform the law, then the solution to our problem and the purpose of Christ must be to enable us to perform the law that we have previously been unable to do. In this model the ultimate goal is still performing the demands of the law, even after the arrival of Jesus Christ. While this is not what we mean when we say these things from our pulpits, the logical end is clear to see. Christ has now become subservient to the law. Since we could never do the law perfectly, God needed to send Jesus to die and rise again so that we could be empowered to follow the law. It is not hard to imagine that many people in our churches would nod in agreement at this formulation.

However, the second problem with this idea is more devastating than the first one. In Philippians 3 Paul boldly and plainly states that he kept the law perfectly. He does not state he has kept the law perfectly after Christ, he stated he kept it perfectly for his whole life. Paul had a zeal for the law that was intense. He ordered his entire existence around keeping all the demands of the Jewish law and spent his life performing every single demand. In our previous formulation, why would Paul even need Jesus Christ? If Christ serves to enable us to follow the law and Paul kept the law perfectly, then Paul would not have needed Jesus Christ in any way.

We are so used to hearing that the problem with the law is that it is impossible to keep it, that this admission by Paul is difficult for most to comprehend. It catches us by surprise. Yet it is plain for all to see. In chapter 3 Paul is writing autobiographically and is demonstrating his Jewish credentials for his readers:

> If someone else thinks they have reasons to put confidence in the flesh, I have more: circumcised on the eighth day, of the people of Israel, of the tribe of Benjamin, a Hebrew of Hebrews; in regard to the law, a Pharisee; as for zeal, persecuting the church; as for righteousness based on the law, faultless" (Phil 3:4–6, NIV).

This is language that should make sense to us after our examination of Romans 5. Paul is not claiming some kind of perfection where he is free of human frailties. This is not his claim at all, rather Paul is stating something far simpler. Paul is claiming that of all the rules and expectations that he knew, he kept all of these without error. Paul never violated the Sabbath, and he kept all of the dietary requirements and food laws. Paul also was keenly aware of all of the regulations that separated the Jewish people as distinct from the gentiles, and not only kept those, but he celebrated them. Paul was proud of his Judaism, and even more proud of his ability to keep the law. If one was a Jew, there was nothing in Paul's life that would have been seen as a failure.

It is possible to read this and perceive this as a boast. That is a fair conclusion because Paul did not lack confidence and was proud of his heritage. It was also the culmination of a larger section that is introduced by imagery of circumcision. This is one of those places where Paul uses the word "flesh" as a code for Jewishness. All of his life Paul had been proud of his Jewish heritage, and he sought to live to its utmost demands. He spent much of his life trying to keep Judaism "pure." Looking back, Paul can state that he kept every law and expectation perfectly. Very few people, if any, can make this statement, but Paul makes it very explicitly.

Many Christians today recoil against this claim. If Paul was perfect, then why did he need to be converted? The answer is refreshingly simple, and we must return to previous chapters for a reminder. Remember Paul's earlier argument from Galatians 3—the law was never intended to be kept as a path to righteousness. Undoubtedly this is not what Jews believed, but Paul had come to learn this after his Damascus Road experience. Paul used to believe that zealously following the law brought righteousness, but this belief was one of those things that died with Paul on the dusty road to Damascus. In Galatians Paul wrote that the purpose of the law was to identify sin, and keep the Jews away from many of its worst effects. If the purpose of the law is to identify sin, and not to make one righteous, then it does not matter if one keeps it perfectly. Paul could have kept it perfectly and found himself no closer to God. This was exactly the experience of Paul, and he knew it intensely as he was struck down on the road to Damascus. For most of his life Paul had viewed the law as an avenue to get closer to the God of Abraham. After the encounter on the road to Damascus, Paul was forced to admit that his real encounter with that God had nothing to do with zealously following the law.

This was a shocking, mid-life correction for Paul that took him years to reformulate. He had spent his life trying to keep all of the law, and suddenly Paul had somehow seen Christ in the middle of that dusty road. In the midst of that experience Paul discovered that his former way of life had been a waste. What was once his highest priority had been discovered to be a loss. The problem was that keeping the law perfectly had brought Paul no closer to God, and the experience that did bring him close had nothing to do with the law at all. This forced Paul to rethink his entire life. It was not surprising that it took Paul more than a decade after his experience on the Damascus Road to launch a public, Christian ministry. When Paul started his ministry, he saw the gentiles experience exactly the same thing that he had. Paul, the ultimate Jew, and pagan gentiles both experienced God in an intimate, life-changing way, and it had nothing to do with the law that Paul had kept perfectly. Everything had fundamentally changed for Paul.

My friend Paul had learned something that he had not thought previously. Until that decisive encounter the law had been everything to Paul. It was the perfect and complete expression of God's will and design for the Jews. This was no longer true, and God's special relationship with humanity was now also with those who were not Jews. The law was still good. The law was moral. The law still had an important role. However, the law did not bring life to those who kept it, even if they kept it perfectly. At best the law brought death to the people that kept it. Paul now knew this, and it made him very unpopular with his former contemporaries. The law can bring moral living, and even perfect performance, but it can never bring life. We correctly think that the law can make humanity good, but that was never the goal. Paul knew something that we can forget. Jesus did not come to make us good. He came that we might have life and have it more abundantly.

This is why Paul's words were so shocking to the Jews. Paul had written that their beloved law actually brings death. It should not surprise us that Paul was never trusted by the Jews, or by the Jewish believers which populated the church in Jerusalem. At the outset of his ministry Paul was clearly not one of the Christian believers. His reputation for persecution was well known. Yet at the end of his ministry the mistrust was still there, but the issue was different. His opponents claimed Paul allowed too many people into the church. He allowed gentiles in without requiring them to keep the law. There were even suspicions that Paul had abandoned the law himself. For all of these reasons he was not to be trusted. Then toward the end of his ministry Paul brought Timothy back to Jerusalem with him and showed him the temple. Those in Jerusalem did not know that Timothy was Jewish. They assumed he was a gentile because he was probably clean shaven like the men in the Greek areas he came from, and because he was there with Paul, the well-known gentile appeaser. Their presence at the temple caused the riot that led to Paul's arrest.

These events only deepened Paul's newfound opinions about the law. The law only served to divide people. The law was the reason the Jews used to exclude the gentiles from the temple and becoming God's people. Pursuit of the law still keeps people away from pursuing God. Maybe the times have not changed that much through the years. When we try to keep the law today the same problems that Paul saw still remain. Perhaps the biggest problem is this idea of perfection. While we preach that no one can keep the law, many of us still pursue this idea of perfection by keeping our own version of the law. Some of us have even learned what Paul did, it is still possible to keep all the rules. It is very possible to have this idea that we are more perfect than others because we have kept the rules better than they have. Yet law keeping is not why God gave the law. The law only serves to point out problems and condemn people. The law was not the solution in Paul's time, and it still is not the answer today. It still alienates, isolates, and leaves us without a solution. My friend Paul discovered this and tried to tell everyone in Philippians 3. Those views got him into trouble then, and I bet it still would.

Caught Between Friends
A Slave and His Patron

PAUL IS ONE OF those figures of history that has left a long and rich legacy. He has been revered in paintings, has been the subject of countless books, and has been granted the status of a saint in the church. We look back at his life from a distance of two thousand years and read his letters in an effort to decipher his advice to us. This is natural and should come as no surprise to us. Yet it is easy to forget that Paul was a real man, who navigated life with real people. He had friends and was often found in difficult positions. Sometimes, these difficult problems led directly to one of his letters. One of the most vexing problems my friend Paul faced was when he found himself stuck between two friends who were dealing with an issue about which many modern people think they know better than Paul, and his solution was reflected in our letter known as the letter to Philemon.

Philemon is one of the least appreciated letters from the hand of Paul. We like to spend time with the richness of Romans, or the social fireworks that are reflected in the letters to the Corinthians. Philemon is much simpler. It is a letter about a friendship triangle, where Paul is friends with two people who are at odds with each other. Paul ends up mediating the issue but does so in a way that serves as a microscope to Paul's larger theology. If we look at how he handled this issue, it will serve to help us understand how Paul formed his theology.

Onesimus was a slave who had left his wealthy patron in Colossae and had gone to be with Paul. We do not know the reasons behind this decision, but we can connect some dots, and re-create the situation with some level of confidence. Onesimus had heard Paul speak and was particularly attracted to Paul's message of freedom in Christ. There was just one problem—Onesimus was a slave. While we do not know what his duties were in Colossae, Onesimus probably lived the routine life of a slave. After hearing Paul speak, he longed to travel with Paul, and be a part of Paul's ministry. From the letter we have it seems that Onesimus was not only talented, but particularly suited for ministry as well. So Onesimus left his routine life as a slave to be with Paul, but it was without the permission or knowledge of Philemon, his patron.

This was a problem for Philemon. He had a household to manage, affairs to consider, and his economic life would have been dependent upon Onesimus, at least in part. Onesimus and Philemon had a common economic arrangement in the Roman Empire, and Onesimus had legal responsibilities to his patron, Philemon. Paul had a relationship with both men, and Paul had a problem on his hands. It seems from the letter that both men were believers, but this problem had the potential to negatively impact the church. This was a problem of status, legal responsibility, but also how status within the church affects the status of life outside the church.

The basic issue is a simple one. Onesimus would like to help Paul, and gain a measure of freedom from his present, cultural condition. He wants to stay with Paul. Philemon would like his slave to be returned, and not suffer an economic loss. Paul wants to strengthen the condition of the church, and have nothing happen that would impact his ministry, or the long-term prospects of the church. Secondarily, Paul would like Onesimus to stay, and become an asset to him in his ministry.

In another sense Paul's first-century problem still spills over into our modern world. We want Paul to say more than he does about slavery. We want him to jump strongly into the political arguments of the twenty-first century, even though he is writing in the first century. Because we want Paul to say more, we end up misreading this entire letter, and that is tragic because this short letter is rich in theology. The modern reader wants Paul to rise to a vigorous defense of Onesimus. We want Paul to write Philemon and tell him that slavery is wrong. We want Paul to write that not only is it wrong but if Philemon expects to be a Christian, he has to end this disgusting practice and free all of his slaves. Nowhere does Paul write any of this, so many look at Paul and charge him with being pro-slavery. Since my friend Paul is supposedly weak on slavery, he is diminished to many modern readers.

Before we leap to that conclusion it might be beneficial to consider if that charge is warranted. We should remember that slavery in the Roman Empire looked nothing like the slavery from our North American experience. In first-century Rome, slavery was common, widespread, and was paid, often paid quite well. There was slavery for common labor, but there were also specialized roles for people who were considered slaves. Philosophers were often hired to entertain at social gatherings. Their role was to entertain the guests by talking about the latest ideas in science and philosophy. These roles were very well paid and enjoyed a high level of social status. We often forget that Plato would have served in a role like this and would have been considered a slave. In many cases slaves held a much higher role in Roman society than a common laborer, like a tent-maker.

We tend to read slavery and our minds immediately go to our own context. This only serves to obscure what is happening in many of Paul's letters. It is quite possible that Paul was offered a position in Corinth as a house-philosopher. He turned it down, and in chapter 7 seemed to encourage other Corinthians to not voluntarily take other slave positions. If Roman slavery was as dark and harsh as we assume, then why would Paul have needed to tell the church in Corinth not to become slaves? The answer is fairly obvious. Slavery was far different in Rome, and was not the racial, forced system that existed in our recent history.

There is one other point to be made here, and it is one that is easy to forget. In the first century slavery simply was. To suggest another type of arrangement would have been confusing. What other system was there? Every culture and every kingdom featured slavery. In an empire like Rome where only 20–30 percent of the people were citizens, slavery was rampant, and was one of the largest portions of society.

Still, there were expectations regarding the practice. While slavery was paid, the slave was bound to their patron, and was expected to finish their commitment. The ancient Greek writer Cicero wrote that a slave could become free after seven years of service, and there were ways where a slave could buy their freedom, but until the term was finished, or the price had been paid, a slave was required to work. There were consequences for abandoning your commitment before the agreed duration. Onesimus had abandoned Philemon, and this created a problem for Paul—a problem that might have extensive repercussions.

Before we let our disappointment with Paul harden, it might be good to take another look at what Paul does say, and as we do, keep the culture of the first century fresh in our minds. The first thing that Paul does is send Onesimus back to Philemon. It is a move that causes many to distrust Paul here. Yet this is not all that Paul does, for he sends Onesimus back with the letter we know as Philemon. Paul writes his friend Philemon and has some very specific words for him. First, Paul affirms Philemon and reminds him of the depth of the relationship he shares with the man. Paul reminds Philemon of how thankful he is for the ministry Philemon has demonstrated. At the end of his plea, Paul also reminds Philemon of how much he owes Paul and says "you owe me your very self." As this reminder brackets Paul's request, Paul writes to Philemon and says to him:

> I am sending him—who is my very heart—back to you. I would have liked to keep him with me so that he could take your place in helping me while I am in chains for the gospel. But I did not want to do anything without your consent, so that any favor you do would not seem forced but would be voluntary. Perhaps the reason he was separated from you for a little while was that you might have him back forever— no longer as a slave, but better than a slave, as a dear brother. He is very dear to me but even

> dearer to you, both as a fellow man and as a brother in
> the Lord." (Phlm 12–16, NIV)

This should be evident to anyone who wishes to take the time and consider our question. Paul is no supporter of slavery. Paul tells Philemon that I could tell you to return him to me, but I want that idea to come from you. Yes, Onesimus is your slave, but there is something better than having a slave in your employment, and that is having a brother by your side. Philemon, I am sending him back, but I expect you to receive him as a brother—a free man. There is Paul's view, and it is plain.

Paul had a dilemma. He had Onesimus with him, but he had left behind a responsibility. Paul had a friendship with Philemon, who had experienced a loss. Paul's view is clear in his answer to Philemon. A brother is better than a slave. In Christ the slave has the same status as the free person. Yet there was a larger goal here—reconciliation. Onesimus cannot really be free as long as Philemon feels he has been wronged. Philemon cannot be free if he feels that Paul has used their friendship for his own gain. As a result of this conundrum, Paul does what he has written about earlier—he demonstrated this ministry of reconciliation.

Then Paul sends Onesimus back, but with this personal plea to Philemon. Take him back but receive him with a new status—as a brother. Then Paul goes one step further. He adds one other thing for Philemon. "If you have been wronged, or if Onesimus owes you anything, add that to my account. I will repay it."

We want Paul to say something different—something that will speak immediately to our modern context, but Paul had a larger issue. Paul wanted to make the situation right for Onesimus and make it right for Philemon as well. In order to facilitate that outcome, Paul stands in between the two men, and offers his own life in return for that outcome. This is not a slogan for Paul, or a political talking point, but it is so much more.

The more important question is, what was the result of this personal plea by Paul? We do not know for certain, but we certainly have clues. In Col 4:9 a person of this name is identified as a Christian accompanying Tychicus to visit the Christians in Colossae.

We also have the strong Christian tradition that an Onesimus was later named bishop of the church in Ephesus and died a martyr's death himself. While we cannot know for certain if that is the same Onesimus, there is a strong possibility that it is. While we want Paul to say more than he does, we should remember that when the NT mentions slavery it is different than our context. While Paul takes a different route, but it is a route that ends with the strong appeal to free Onesimus, and an Onesimus that is welcomed by his employer as a brother.

This is still not the answer many would like today, but Paul's day is not today. Slavery was a practice that simply was, and it was universally practiced. One could wish Paul to make a strong political stance to satisfy modern demands, and perhaps end with an appeal to set up a capitalistic or socialistic system. The problem is that neither of these had even been expressed yet and would serve only to impose our political concerns back onto the text.

Paul was not concerned with our politics, and probably not as concerned with his as we would like. Paul was concerned with the dynamics within the church, and the approaching kingdom of God. His wish is that people would live with their ultimate concern being their place in the kingdom of Christ, and not their place in the empire of Rome.

Paul's answer is still instructive. He literally stands between Onesimus and Philemon and does all he can to make it right. He does not seek to make it right politically, and then impose that change from the top. Rather he stands with these men and seeks to offer reconciliation. We should also notice that Paul refers to a personal history of which we are not aware. In his letter to Philemon Paul reminds Philemon that "he owes (Paul) his very life." We do not know about the events surrounding this claim, but we can be sure that both Philemon and Paul do. With this history in mind, Paul uses it as pressure to apply to Philemon. Using that pressure Paul urges him to accept Onesimus as a brother. Yet there is still a danger. If Philemon still feels wronged then reconciliation is still not possible, so Paul makes a personal guarantee. If this arrangement means you are owed something, then Paul assures him that he will repay that debt himself. Paul's answer is place himself between the debtor and the one to whom the debt is owed, and pay the penalty himself.

Where would Paul have found this kind of plan? The answer is obvious—he learned it from the example of Christ. Christ assumed a debt that he did not owe so he could offer his life to reconcile us to God. With this example in mind, my friend Paul does the same thing for Onesimus and Philemon. He offered his life to reconcile these two friends. It is not the political answer we want today, but it is a powerful one that still resonates today, and it springs from Paul.

A Living Corpse?

The Nature of the Resurrection

WE DO NOT UNDERSTAND how difficult a task Paul faced. The early believers in Christ were all Jewish, so they shared a common background and understanding of the world. That all changed when Paul took this new faith to the gentiles. The difficulty of Paul's task was at least doubled. He not only had to explain that Jesus was the Son of God, he had to explain to the gentiles the Jewish understanding of God as well. The common background of the early believers was absent in places like Corinth, which complicated the task of taking Jesus to the whole world.

Paul had spent a long time in Corinth, roughly eighteen months, and spent the majority of that time teaching the new believers and establishing the new church there. After Paul left, he received a letter from Chloe that asked Paul a series of questions. His answers to these questions comprise a large portion of 1 Corinthians. In 1 Cor 7:1 we read Paul's response to the church in Corinth: "Now for the matters you wrote me about." The remainder of 1 Corinthians is half of a conversation between Paul and his church. While we do not know the exact questions that the Corinthians gave to Paul, we can make an educated guess about the questions by reading Paul's answers.

In chapter 15 Paul answered a question about the resurrection. In 15:35 Paul acknowledges the question he has been asked: "Someone will ask, how are the dead raised?" While we do not know the exact nature of the issue, we do know that for the

Corinthians, the resurrection was a problem. This can strike us as odd, because we cannot understand why the heart of the Christian good news would ever be a problem. We look forward to going to heaven, we sing about it in a number of our hymns and wonder what the problem with heaven could be. Yet there was something in Paul's teaching that caused a real and lingering problem for the believers in Corinth.

If a Christian today goes to an average funeral, they might hear a common message. "Brother Jim did not die without hope. He believed in Jesus Christ and served Christ for much of his life. So, we know that Jim is in heaven today. His soul has gone to be with the Lord. If we live faithfully, we can someday join brother Jim in heaven." While this is a common message in many funerals today, we know this is *not* the message that Paul preached in Corinth. We know this because the people of Corinth would have understood this presentation of death well, because it is a completely Greek idea of death. This is not what Paul preached, and because Paul's message was new, the Corinthians had trouble understanding what Paul was preaching. If Paul preached the same message he shared in Corinth with us today, we would have the same issues that the Corinthians had.

The ancient Greek world understood the world in a Platonic way. In other words, they thought about the world in a strong, dualistic manner. The Greeks divided the world into material and non-material categories. This dualistic view of the world was quite common then. For Greeks the non-material was always to be favored over the material. The material world was seen as deficient, if not outright evil. The non-material, or spirit world, stood in sharp contrast to the material world. The spirit world was pure, and not stained with the material of the physical world.

This affected how the Greeks viewed the divine. Everything that is good or holy to a Greek involved the non-physical. Therefore, if Paul had merely preached that upon death, our souls go to heaven to dwell with God they would have wholeheartedly received that message, for it would have been a thoroughly Greek idea. Yet that is not what Paul had told them. Paul had preached the Christian idea of a bodily resurrection. It is not just the soul that goes to heaven, but the entire person that will be raised from the dead. This was Paul's message, and it caused an immediate problem.

It seems that this was not the good news in Corinth that Paul thought it would be. Instead of hearing resurrection of the dead, some Corinthians heard Paul's message as "resuscitation of the corpse." This was not the good news that Paul thought it was. The Corinthians thought that their material body had been a problem all of their lives, and now that death had come, why would they want to drag it around even longer than they needed to? They longed to be free from the body, not sentenced to an even longer time with it.

At times in our recent past, we have not been too far from the Corinthians. We have spoken about going to heaven, or our soul leaving the body. We speak of going to heaven and looking down upon all of the friends and family who remain behind. This is a natural response to the loss that death represents, and one that is found across many cultures. While all of this is natural and under-standable, it is mainly a reminder of our Greek heritage, and is not our Christian hope. My friend Paul walked into this Greek culture and told them that the body was not evil. It was a part of God's good creation, and it will be redeemed as well. Therefore, for Paul, the resurrection is not a spirit event, but an event that involves the whole person. That news was not received as well as Paul would have liked.

Paul could have pulled back part of his message at this point and simply affirmed what we so often affirm, that when we die our soul would simply leave our body and go to heaven, but he never did. For Paul there was too much at stake. Giving up the claim that the resurrection involves the body would have sacrificed the heart of our Christian message, and that was too steep of a price for Paul. In chapter 15 Paul is forced to re-approach the resurrection, and to do so in a way that will satisfy the questions of those in Corinth.

When those in Corinth first heard Paul's message they were taken aback by Paul's claim. Given their negative feelings toward all things material, the Corinthians heard Paul's words about resurrection, and thought Paul was talking about resuscitation of a corpse. The thought of continued life in a body that was already subject to decay and death was not pleasant, and they naturally recoiled. They wanted a further clarification, so they asked Paul what he meant. Paul's answer in chapter 15 tried to stay faithful to the heart of the Christian message, while relieving the concerns of the Corinthians. If we take a renewed look at Paul's words in Corinthians, it just might relieve some of our modern confusion about the resurrection.

First, Paul wholeheartedly embraced a bodily resurrection. While the Corinthians objected to that for their reasons, we tend to do the same thing for our own reasons. We are so used to the normal processes of life, and the reality of aging, that we have a hard time conceiving of this as well. What period of life will we look like with our resurrected bodies? What happens to those who die in explosive or fiery accidents and there is little left of the body? What about those children who die minutes after their birth? We have a hard time imagining what that will look like, so we speak in generalities of going to heaven.

The other issue that we have is a time element. We so want to imagine our loved one still being with us, that we resort to a disembodied soul still living and looking down on us. We think this even as we watch the body being lowered into the grave. It is times like these, the old words of "Our sure and certain hope of the resurrection" should ring true. Yet we have lost this affirmation of the bodily resurrection in our own time as well. There is much at stake if we lose this important distinction.

In order to address these concerns Paul uses some simple concepts to affirm this important concept. Paul affirmed that there is a resurrection body, and that it is firmly connected to our physical bodies. He uses the metaphor of seeds in verse 37 to emphasize this. Paul tells the Corinthians that they are too fixated on their earthly bodies. Whatever the reality will be, what we are now is only a seed. In our own language a majestic oak tree is not an acorn, but everything needed for that oak is contained in the acorn. For the acorn to become an oak, the acorn must die, and so it is with us. What we will be is so much greater than what we are now, but we will never know that reality unless we die.

This is also language of continuity for Paul. While an acorn transforms into an oak tree, an acorn will never produce a maple tree. For that one needs the whirling action of a maple seed. With this simple metaphor Paul is telling these Greeks that the resurrection will feature a body that is particular to them, will be known by others, but will be completely transformed from what we know in this life. In other words, Paul said, "do not concern yourself too much with what has been here, for God has something far greater in store." It is unique, it is physical, but it is transformative as well.

Here is why a bodily resurrection was so important to Paul, and every Christian from Paul's time until now. Without the bodily resurrection there is no defeat of sin. The promise of Isaiah is not that your soul will float to heaven, but that "They will soar on wings like eagles; they will run and not grow weary, they will walk and not be faint." When sin and death deprive us of our ability to walk, speak, or embrace one another, a bodiless resurrection is nice, but it restores or reverses nothing at all. When an evil tyrant threatens us with death, or extreme physical torture, the bodily resurrection is the promise that no tyrant can ever take away anything good that God created. The early church did not walk into the arena with the hope that the soul would live on, they walked with confidence and the full assurance that they would indeed, walk, run, and embrace the ones they love again.

Many of us have friends that have been severely impacted by trial and physical hardship, and while we do not often think about the consequences of a bodily resurrection, these people do. There is a friend of mine who was born with cerebral palsy. There has never been a day in her life where she has taken a step without worrying about balance or the daily reality of falling down. There has never been a day where she has run, or given a full, bear-hug embrace. Such an action would prove to be too painful. I am sure she would have loved to have children, or pursue a romantic relationship, but none have happened. This is not because of any failure on her part, but all are a direct result of the disease she has known all of her life. The resurrection of the body tells my friend she will run and not grow weary, she will walk and not lose her balance. If the soul is all that survives then sin wins, and so does its sibling, death. If heaven is only a place to where the soul ascends then tyrants that kill and maim can take away what God has created. This is not the victory to which Paul testified.

My friend Paul knew this in a visceral way. The power of Rome was a daily reality. Rome could arrest, imprison and kill anyone. Occasionally, Paul saw the grisly results of crucifixions during his travels. He remembered the Roman encampments around his boyhood home of Tarsus and remembered their power. He also thought about his message, and the threat that was perceived by the authorities. The powers of Rome could end Paul's life someday, and Paul knew it. After all, Paul proclaimed a Messiah that Rome had previously killed. Paul knew what was at stake. Here was a man subject to arrest, floggings, and severe beatings. The bodily resurrection was not an academic exercise for my friend Paul, it was a daily hope and comfort. It was a comfort because even though he proclaimed a crucified Messiah, he proclaimed one that had defeated death as well—physically. Perhaps we have lost some of that hope. During those eighteen months in Corinth, Paul was trying to make the believers there a little less Greek, and a lot more Christian. Perhaps we should do the same.

Second Class

Paul and Women

It would be hard to imagine a more traditional environment than a conservative Jewish home. While that statement is true today, it would have been even more true in the first century. This also would have been true even in the Greek culture around Asia Minor. It was expected in a traditional Greek home that the husband would make all the decisions of the home. His wife would have been expected to raise the children, be a good hostess, and provide an admirable environment for the family. Beyond these simple expectations, there was not much else available for a Greek woman. The same would be true of a Jewish family. Men were expected to rule the family, and women played a clearly subservient role. Women were not expected or allowed to lead, and their role in Jewish society was very limited.

Even though the men were expected to lead in both Jewish and Greek homes, there were distinct differences between these cultures. In a Greek home, sexual fidelity was not an expectation for the Greek patriarch. Sexual expression could be found elsewhere, whether in the presence of other women or even younger boys. As Plato's *Symposium* makes clear, the ideal sexual partner for a Greek male was a pubescent boy. In a Jewish home fidelity was expected to accompany the responsibilities of leadership. Devotion to the family was an expectation in Jewish homes that did not exist to the same extent in Greek culture, but in both cultures, the males were expected to lead.

Some of Paul's words in the New Testament have been used to support the continuation of some of this culture even in our own time. In Eph 5:22 Paul has words for the believers in Asia Minor. He writes, "Wives, submit to your husbands." These words have been used to support a very traditional arrangement in homes across cultures, and across centuries. This is proof, it is said, that my friend Paul supported male prominence not only in homes, but in the broader church as well.

This is not a controversial statement. Some modern writers even look back on Paul and declare him to be a misogynist and use his words here as evidence. This is not the only evidence for this charge against Paul. In 1 Corinthians 14 Paul also wrote that women are to be silent in his churches. Such direct and harsh language might have been more common in the first century, but with today's values Paul looks very negative toward women indeed. Yet what if we have misread Paul at a foundational level? While we must remember that Paul was a man trapped in his own time, there might be clues from that time and place that would cause a fair reader to reassess the words, and ideas of my friend Paul.

In Eph 5:21 Paul writes what is known as a household code, or *haustafel* to the believers in Asia Minor. While this sounds new to us, a household code was actually a very common literary device in the ancient world. This type of code was a basic set of instructions on how the family unit, and wider culture should be constructed. Cicero wrote a famous household code, as did Plato, and a host of other Greek writers as well. All of them had a stake in how the larger culture would be designed, and all of them followed a similar pattern in what was written. Every Greek household code was written to the patriarch of the family. It gave the patriarch instructions and told him how to relate to every other unit within his household. There were instructions about wives, about how to raise and relate to the children, and instructions on relations with any slaves that were in the home as well. In short, the patriarch was to rule over the family, and command every aspect of the home. In fact, the entirety of the household code was written to the patriarch of the home. He was the one person in the home who counted, and every bit of instruction was written solely to the male head.

Against this background we can judge Paul's words in Ephesians in a new light. While Paul writes in the pattern of a familiar household code, his words are a radical departure from the other codes of that time. In every other household code, the patriarch of the family was the sole person addressed. It was a guide to relate how the patriarch was to relate to every other part of the household. In the male-dominated culture, the only person worthy of address was the male head of the household.

Not so with Paul. He addressed not only the head of the household, but every other member within the household as well. This is a radical departure for a writer of the first century. Paul considered the wife, the children, and the slave all worthy of personal interaction, and he wrote to each part of the ancient home. This would have been scandalous in the first century. On this basis alone Paul was not the misogynist that some people claim.

Yet we should also take a look at the actual words of Paul within his household code and see how these would have been heard in the first century. It is surprising how often our reading of Paul starts with Eph 5:22 and the instruction for wives to submit, while we ignore the introductory verse immediately preceding it—"submit to one another out of reverence for Christ." Every other Greek writer wrote to the patriarch instructing them to rule over their households, while Paul begins with equal instruction to both spouses. The implication was clear. The success of the household was completely dependent upon the decisions of the male head. The first instruction of Paul to the male head of household was to also submit to his wife. We read the following verse and wonder if Paul hates women. The ancient reader would have read the first verse and would have considered him to be weak. A male does not submit. A male rules over his household.

There are numerous examples that show the prevailing opinion of Greek culture on women. The ancient Greek writer Arius Didymus argued that "a man has the rule of this household by nature, for the deliberative faculty in a woman is inferior, in children it does not yet exist, and in the case of slaves, it was completely absent."[1] Josephus stated, "the woman, says the Law, is in all things inferior to the man. Let her accordingly be submissive, not for her humiliation, but that she may be directed; for the authority has been given by God to the man."[2] Aristotle may have said it even more convincingly:

> Of household management we have seen that there are three parts—one is the rule of a master over slaves. . . another of a father, and the third of a husband. A husband and father rules over wife and children, both free, but the rule differs, the rule over his children being a royal, over his wife a constitutional rule. For although there may be exceptions to the order of nature, the male is by nature fitter for command than the female. . . . For the slave has no deliberative faculty at all; the woman has, but it is without authority, and the child has, but it is immature. So it must necessarily be with the moral virtues also; all may be supposed to partake of them, but only in such manner and degree as is required by each for the fulfillment of his duty.[3]

These are clear examples of the wider Greek culture, and the role of women within that culture.

Paul's words about submission immediately stand in stark contrast to the wider Greek culture. Yet Paul's instruction goes even further than mutual submission. In more pointed words Paul commands men to love their wives, and to sacrifice for their well-being. While we nod approvingly at these words today, we have lost sight of how revolutionary these words would have been in the Greek culture of the first century. These words would have clearly stood in sharp contrast to the culture of Paul's day. Paul does not only address women, but he also addressed children and slaves as well. When Paul directly addressed people that are not used to being addressed there is a bold message being delivered. With Christ

---

1 Aristotle, *Politics* 1.12.

2 *Against Apion* 2.199.

3 Aristotle, *Politics,* parts 12–13.

women, children and slaves have value, and all are worthy to be followers.

Paul seems to have understood this and included women in other unexpected ways. In Gal 3:28 Paul writes that "in Christ, there is neither . . male nor female." This is not praise for a certain androgyny, but a simple recognition that the things that separate us in the world will not do so in the church. In Rom 16:1, Paul calls Phoebe a servant, which is also how he described himself. In 16:7 Paul also called Junias a fellow apostle. In the closing chapter of Romans Paul elevates women to the same status that he describes himself. This description would have been very surprising to that culture.

The question that some ask is, where would have Paul found the possibility for such a change? The answer is within his own Judaism. The prophet Joel had looked ahead to the coming day of the Lord in the Old Testament and said, "Even on my servants, both men and women, I will pour out my Spirit in those days." (2:29) As Paul traveled through the empire preaching the gospel, he noticed something else. God was reaching men and women. His Spirit was being poured out on Jew and gentile, slave and free, men and women. The days promised centuries earlier were happening in Paul's time. For Paul the role of women was not an academic issue, but proof from his native Judaism that God's promised kingdom was already arriving.

All of this does not stop modern readers from seeing Ephesians 5:22–6:9 as being unduly restrictive on women. Some look to other texts as well in support of their view that Paul has a problem with women. The text mentioned more than any other is probably 1 Cor 14:34, where Paul commands women to be silent in the church. This is another verse that many believe shows that Christianity is anti-women at its core. Unfortunately, it is a passage that has also been used by some in the church to enforce a diminished role for women in our midst. Again, to the modern ear this sounds plainly anti-woman, but we should be reminded this was not written to our time.

It is hard to appreciate the type of place that Corinth was during the first century. It was a relatively new city, full of vitality and new wealth. It was a destination for recently freed slaves and was situated at the crossroads of the Empire. It was located on the Isthmus of Corinth and had a port on both its east and west sides. Since the Peloponnesian peninsula was to its south, it was problematic to transport goods via ship all the way around to the opposite coast. Instead, ships would dock at the port on the east side of Corinth, transport goods overland a few miles to the west side, and place them on another ship. This not only saved time but placed Corinth at a strategic location. If immorality arrived when the fleet came in, we should remember that Corinth had twice that activity with its opposing ports on both sides of town.

Corinth was also famous for another reason—it was a religious center of its day. Home to over ten pagan temples, people came to Corinth from all over the empire to worship at its temples. From the powerful Apollo to Asklepios, the god of healing, Corinth was at the center of religious life. In many of these temples, women were at the heart of the worship experience, in ways both good and harmful. In the temple to Aphrodite hundreds of women served as temple prostitutes. Since this was a temple to the god of beauty, we should not be surprised that the "worship" experience involved ritualized prostitution. In other temples women served as priestesses who consulted the gods and delivered the oracles from those gods to the people. In another temple, the one dedicated to Demeter, the women led worship, and that worship was both enthusiastic and ecstatic.

We should not be surprised to discover that if this varied pagan background was ongoing in Corinth, and as new people were coming into this church, they brought some of their religious practices and expectations with them. We like it when new people come to church, but if in the middle of reading Scripture, a formerly woman priest from Demeter stands up with her shaved head and begins displaying some ecstatic behavior, the new church may have a problem. This would be especially true if a sizable portion of the church was Jewish, or this fledgling body of believers already had established practices. It is highly possible that these words to women in Corinth were referencing specific behaviors that were causing a problem. The readers knew what those were, but we have two thousand years of distance between these words and us. If these words directed at women in Corinth were to be universally understood, then one would expect to find them in Paul's other letters as well, especially Romans, since Paul has time to collect his thoughts and write all that he considered important. The fact that we do not find this is perhaps instructive to us.

There is one other vital piece of evidence that we rarely notice. Paul largely writes what he does in Corinthians because he is answering a letter he has already received from them. In 1 Corinthians 7 Paul plainly states, "Now for the matters you wrote about. . ." Yet in chapter 1 Paul writes from whom these questions came. They came from Chloe. We do not know exactly who Chloe was, but she was either the patron of the church and hosted this fellowship, or she was a leader of this church. Either way Chloe was a person of importance to this church. This is important. When we consider the words of 1 Corinthians 14, the fact that Chloe is a person of importance should restrict us from the idea that Paul is proposing that women be banned from leadership. Context is everything, but context is what many modern readers fail to understand.

Many people today diminish Paul as an ancient, woman-hating Jew. That is an easy claim to make looking back with two thousand year old hindsight, but such a claim would surprise my friend Paul. Looking back in the comfort of modern views, Paul seems like a man out of touch with the expectations of modern women. Yet Paul did not exist in our time. In the time of the first century Paul had some rather radical views, and inclusion of women was one of them. We have trouble noticing this, but the Jews and Greeks of the first century would have noticed.

Too Wonderful

A Life-Changing Experience

EVEN AFTER YEARS OF his public, Christian ministry, what happened to Paul on that road to Damascus never left his mind. It was an event that completely changed his life, but he still struggled to explain it. It was so wonderful and life-changing for Paul, words completely failed him. There was a time when Paul tried to explain what had happened, but it only served to confuse people, and it still does. 2 Corinthians 12:2–6 states:

> I know a man in Christ who fourteen years ago was caught up to the third heaven. Whether it was in the body or out of the body I do not know—God knows. And I know that this man—whether in the body or apart from the body I do not know, but God knows—was caught up to paradise and heard inexpressible things, things that no one is permitted to tell. I will boast about a man like that, but I will not boast about myself, except about my weaknesses." (NIV)

This is a hard passage to understand as it is filled with terms that are unique to this passage. It starts with this description of a "third heaven." The "third heaven" is a strange concept to us today that raises all sorts of questions. Are there different levels of heaven? Do different levels of heaven correspond to how well one has lived; the more good works the higher the level, with "death bed" conversions being at the bottom, and lifelong saints occupying the highest level? What exactly is "the third heaven"?

These are understandable questions for modern people, who have an established, scientific view of the Earth. Most of us have lived in a world where we have seen a picture of Earth taken from the surface of the moon. This informs our understanding in ways we do not consciously appreciate. This verse is a good example of how two thousand years and a different culture can come between the text and our understanding of what Paul was trying to say. If we were a part of his Jewish culture two thousand years ago this sentence would have made more sense than it does to us today.

First, most students of Scripture accept that Paul is writing this verse about himself, and that he is referring to his own visionary experience on the road to Damascus some years earlier (Acts 9:1–9, 22:6–11). It was this experience that caused Paul to claim in another letter that he had seen the risen Christ (1 Cor 15:1–10, cf. Gal 1:12). Some people have been thrown off the trail by Paul's words of another man, but his half-hearted attempt at modesty in addressing the Corinthians did not fool his first readers and should not fool us either. Well, the man that Paul described was himself. He was not trying to be deceitful or evasive but used this method of writing as a means of getting his point across in the letter.

Remember that there was a group in Corinth, maybe even the majority, who were questioning the authority of Paul (1 Cor 9:1–14, 2 Cor 10–11). This group was following the lead of some who were claiming higher knowledge due to some special powers or ecstatic experience (1 Cor 12; cf. 1 Cor 3:21, 4:6–7). It could be that after diminishing the importance of these "powers" that Paul did not want to use his own special experience to claim authority for himself, even though he admits just a few verses later that he was the man he was describing (12:7). His point was to establish his authority as an apostle without boasting about his own spiritual experiences to do so (cf. 12:5). This all simply suggests that the answer to the identity of the third heaven will come from within this text and its historical context and not from our own later theological or scientific ideas that are separated from the culture of the original audience.

Jews of that time did not have the scientific knowledge that we take for granted, so they did not think of the world in scientific terms or descriptions. Instead, they attempted to conceptualize the world in terms of what they knew, and usually described it visually. So, when they conceived of the universe, they constructed a multi-layered world, sort of like a large onion composed of various layers with the physical world in which human beings lived at the center. These layers were called "firmament" or *shamayim* (heavens or sky) in the Old Testament or "heavens" in the New Testament era. There are many other non-Biblical books and writings that also describe these layers. This model was still in use in the Middle Ages (AD 1400s) when Dante wrote of the various levels of heaven and hell in the *Divine Comedy*. There were many ancient descriptions where seven layers of heaven were described but in other writings there were only three layers. When Paul uses this concept of a third heaven, it sounds strange to us, but it would have been familiar to his early readers.

Even though the number of layers was different these models of the universe shared some common traits. The lowest heaven, the core of the "onion," is the visible physical world that all people can see. In most of these models the second heaven is composed of water, a great sea, a firmament dividing the earth from the heavenly beings. This water that surrounded the earth became a common symbol for chaos and disorder that threatened to engulf the world. So often, these waters were understood to be gathered to await the coming day of judgment when they would once again be loosed to destroy the unrighteous. This seems strange to us, but it is a perfectly understandable response that ancient cultures would have understood. An ancient person could walk to the edge of land and look out over the vast expanse of blue waters. That same person could then look up and see that same color in the sky. Later, a storm would come, and this same person would observe water falling from the sky at the same time as thunder and lightning fumble and flash in an effort to tear the sky apart. The simple observation that sky and sea were made of the same material would be a natural assumption. It is an assumption shared in the creation story when God separated the waters above from the waters below and called them "sky" and "sea."

However, the third heaven was beyond the sight of human beings. It was the dwelling place of God and his attendant heavenly beings whom he would send to protect Israel and the righteous. Therefore, when Paul claims to have seen the risen Christ he is describing his experience in terms that he, and others, would readily understand. In that cultural context, he would have assumed that God had taken him to the region where it was possible to see spiritual beings, and the risen Christ. In modern language Paul saying he had seen the third heaven was equivalent to saying he had seen God in a vision. In modern terms he was describing an event so wonderful that words failed him. It was not often that words failed my friend Paul, but this experience was one of those times.

On his way to Damascus, Paul had everything figured out. He knew his beloved Judaism and the places where his people failed to uphold the law. Paul also knew his role in defending this faith. There were very few people who could match Paul's level of training or understanding, and Paul knew it. His self-assurance was based on years of study, and other Jews were comforted by Paul's confidence. It would have been hard to imagine Paul changing his mind about his Jewish heritage. Some friends thought it would take an act of God for Paul to change. Then came that trip to Damascus and the words to describe that encounter were hard to come by.

Understanding this takes nothing away from Paul's own testimony of an encounter with God. It simply acknowledges that Paul was a child of his day, that he lived in a pre-scientific world that had its own views of expressing and depicting the makeup of the physical world. When given the chance Paul described his experiences in the only way that he had at hand. His point was not to tell us how many levels of heaven there might really be. His point was to tell us that he had powerfully encountered the presence of God, in fact that he had physically seen the risen Christ. That fact is not directly related to the manner in which Paul tells us about that experience; the point is that it happened, and it made a pivotal difference in Paul's life.

The Spirit
The Heart of Christianity

IN AN EARLIER CHAPTER we discussed Paul's argument in Romans 7, and whether his words were meant to be read from the perspective of the experience of an individual, or a larger group. At the end of that previous chapter, we were reminded about the hopeless place we find ourselves in the following words of Paul: "Who will deliver me from this body of death?" The despairing tone of chapter 7 makes the opening words of chapter 8 sound even more triumphant. "There is therefore no condemnation for those who are in Christ Jesus." These words are not a surprise to us and are a natural response to the hopeless end of chapter 7. Of course, Jesus Christ is the answer to the hopelessness in chapter 7. We expect Paul to launch into an extended discussion on the death of Jesus Christ, and the importance of the cross, but that is not what Paul does. At this triumphant point, Paul does not talk about the cross, but about the Spirit. We should not miss this point, especially those of us who embrace a holiness ethic, but I fear that we do miss this point.

Many Christians would expect a discussion about the cross and redemption here. We are in this hopeless estate because we owe a debt that we cannot pay. Jesus came to Earth to take our place and pay our debt. Because of this sacrifice, we are freed from the penalty of sin. This would be the argument that most believers would make today, but surprisingly this is not the argument that Paul made. It is at this crucial juncture that Paul launches into a lengthy discussion about the Spirit. Even in the Christian traditions that emphasizes the role of the Spirit, many might relegate the Spirit to a discussion that centers on a certain secondary work of grace. Yet for Paul the Spirit is primary, and the linchpin of his argument resides at the climax of the book of Romans. This is why this discussion has been saved for the end of the book. This discussion could have followed our earlier discussion of Romans 7, but the Spirit is primary for Paul.

We should remember that Paul's entire thought world had been turned upside down on the road to Damascus. His whole life had been dedicated to the pursuit of the law, and the primacy of the Jewish religious life. Yet that world crumbled on the dusty road to Damascus where Paul had experienced a transforming encounter with God. Then during his travels around the Empire, my friend Paul saw other people experience the same thing that he had. While his previous life had been dedicated to the preservation of Judaism, God was now reaching gentiles as well. If the gentiles were coming to Christ in large numbers, the law could not be the primary force that Paul had previously thought. If the law was no longer the primary expression of God's work in the world, what now is? This crucial role would be filled by the Spirit.

This was no plan B forced on Paul by the strange events that started on his journey to Damascus. With his life-long devotion to Judaism, and the expectations that the Pharisees had for the Messiah, Paul was an expert in the Scriptures. In the heart of those Scriptures was an expectation of what would happen when the Lord intervened in history. Joel 2:27–29 stated:

> Then you will know that I am in Israel, that I am the Lord your God, and that there is no other; never again will my people be shamed. And afterward, I will pour out my Spirit on all people. Your sons and daughters will prophesy, your old men will dream dreams, your young men will see visions. Even on my servants, both men and women, I will pour out my Spirit in those days. (NIV)

When Paul was left blinded on the road all those years before, he was forced to reconsider what he thought he knew. The longer

Paul served, and the more journeys Paul undertook, only served to bring events into a sharper focus for him. The future which he had formally anticipated at the end of history was happening in the middle of Paul's life, and the presence of the Spirit proved it. This was the culmination of the promise given to the prophet centuries before. Before his very eyes, the Spirit was being poured out in places like Corinth and Philippi, and Jews and gentiles alike were coming to Christ. This was not some sidelight for Paul, but the full culmination of God's promise.

This probably also explains why Paul was so steadfast in his defense of these gentiles. To some of his former Jewish friends, Paul defense of these gentiles must have looked like a betrayal to Judaism. Yet for Paul the inclusion of the gentiles was the climax to his beloved Judaism. Wasn't Abraham promised that he would be the father of many nations? Did not God promise that he would bless all people through Abraham? Through their zealous regard for the law, the Jews believed that promise, but only imagined that the people blessed would be Jewish. Then the prophet promised that God's Spirit would come to Jew and gentile alike. This was the central promise of Judaism, and somehow my friend Paul had been chosen to take Christ to these gentiles, and then defend their role in this new church.

Here are Paul's triumphant words that open chapter 8:

> Therefore, there is now no condemnation for those who are in Christ Jesus, because through Christ Jesus the law of the Spirit who gives life has set you free from the law of sin and death. For what the law was powerless to do because it was weakened by the flesh, God did by sending his own Son in the likeness of sinful flesh to be a sin offering. And so he condemned sin in the flesh, in order that the righteous requirement of the law might be fully met in us, who do not live according to the flesh but according to the Spirit.
>
> Those who live according to the flesh have their minds set on what the flesh desires; but those who live in accordance with the Spirit have their minds set on what the Spirit desires. The mind governed by the flesh is death,

but the mind governed by the Spirit is life and peace.
(Rom 8:1–6, NIV)

We should remember at this point of our discussion where Paul left us at the end of chapter 7. "Who will rescue me from this body of death?" This was Paul's cry at the end of chapter 7, and he was representing all of those who strive to live according to the law. Since the law was only intended to identify sin and condemn it fully, those who try to live according to the law will only find condemnation. They will find condemnation not because they failed, but because the law succeeded in its intended role. Since the whole point of the law is to bring condemnation, even faithfulness to the law will only leave us where the law intended to take us. This is why Paul is so despairing at the end of seven, but also why my friend Paul was so triumphant in chapter 8. There is another way to live, and it was a way that the Old Testament predicted—the Spirit.

This idea was not a new idea for Paul. It was an idea he returned to again and again in his letters. The problem with the law was that it was always intended to be temporary. Therefore, when believers tried to return to the ways of the law, they were building on temporary foundations. Their lives could not be complete, because the goal of the Jewish law was never meant to be obedience to that law, but to use the law to point the way to Christ. There was another way to live, and it was the way of the Spirit. For Paul the divide was not as much law vs Christ, as it was law versus Spirit.

The choice for believers was simple. While the law was temporary, the Spirit is active and continuing. It was the Spirit that was the definitive proof for Paul that God was indeed, doing a new thing. Later in 8:11 Paul wrote, "if the Spirit of him who raised Jesus from the dead is living in you, he who raised Christ from the dead will also give life to your mortal bodies because of his Spirit who lives in you." This was a Spirit who gave life, and it stood in stark contrast to the law, which only brought death. 2 Corinthians 3:6 was even more pronounced on this subject. "He has made us competent as ministers of a new covenant—not of the letter but of the Spirit; for the letter kills, but the Spirit gives life." Not only had the prophets told us about this coming Spirit, but Jesus had promised the Spirit as well. Paul was a witness to both Jew and gentile and their reception of the promised Holy Spirit. Too often, these new believers were often too quick to abandon this new way of life, just to return to the familiar depictions of the law.

Time and time again Paul faced this recurring problem, and it was his most common struggle. In Romans, Paul wrote to this church he had not founded, did not know personally and gave them the heart of his message. Everything that the law described could be faithfully lived, but not by trying to follow the dictates of the law. Instead, we were to rely on the Spirit. Romans 8 is Paul's most detailed attempt to describe how to do this. The holy life that the law described was available to those who stayed in an active relationship with the Spirit. We must have our mind in agreement with the Spirit, and our daily walk must match that same Spirit. Whenever we cut ourselves off from the Spirit, we place ourselves in jeopardy.

In certain traditions throughout history there have been those who have diminished the role of the Spirit to a one-time emotional experience, but not Paul. For Paul the Spirit was a daily source of strength for the believer. The presence of the Holy Spirit was nothing less than the central focus of the Christian life. There was nothing second about the Spirit in the mind of Paul. The Spirit was the primary evidence for God's work in the world, the down payment we are given for eternal life and the primary source of strength and guidance for the church and each individual believer. The Spirit was everything for Paul.

The language that Paul used in chapter 8 is important. It is the language of a continuing journey. The Spirit is one that lives in us, and we allow that presence to guide and control our actions. In chapter 8 we are not called to make a decision or seek an experience, but to daily live and be led by that Spirit. In Gal 5:25 we are told to keep in step with the Spirit. This language evokes images of a walk. Our pace and direction must match the direction which God shows us, and we must match the pace of the Spirit's direction. Far more than a one-time event this is an active and dynamic presence that accompanies us in every endeavor of life.

There is one other place where the Spirit was prominent for Paul, and it is a place that confuses many modern commentators today. In Gal 4:6 Paul wrote, "Because you are his sons, God sent the Spirit of his Son into our hearts, the Spirit who calls out, *"Abba, Father."* So you are no longer a slave, but God's child; and since you are his child, God has made you also an heir" (NIV).

We should remember the issue that was confusing the church in Galatia. After Paul had left, there were those representing the church in Jerusalem who followed Paul and told the new believers in Galatia that Paul was a good guy, but his message of the gospel was inadequate and incomplete. Yes, we come to Christ through faith, but anyone who wanted to be a part of God's people had to also listen to Genesis 17, and its message that every male needed to be circumcised. From Paul's words in Galatians, it seemed that many of the new believers volunteered for circumcision. This act seems like devotion to many, but for Paul it was a basic betrayal of the gospel. In response to this practice, Paul wrote the letter to the Galatians, and specifically these words from chapter 4.

When we read, "Abba, Father" in Gal 4:6, most people immediately go to the words of Jesus on the cross in Mark. While that is a natural place to go, it is difficult to see how Paul goes from there to the issue at hand in Galatia. Yet this is not the only time these words are used. When Isaac accompanied his father to the top of Mt. Moriah in Genesis 22, he says the same words in asking his father, "Where is the ram for the sacrifice?" This is a vital distinction. At the time the New Testament was written, Isaac was the person who was the focal point of that story in Genesis. He was the obedient son, the willing sacrifice and he was strongly linked with the activity of God's Spirit which fits in well with Paul's main point.

Paul is telling his readers that Isaac was the son of the promise and was linked with the Spirit. Ishmael was not the son of the promise, having been the result of Abraham's interactions with Hagar. After the birth of Isaac, Abraham circumcised both sons—Ishmael, who was thirteen at the time, and Isaac as a baby. The age of thirteen is important to the Jews. It is the age when a boy becomes a man and becomes responsible for the law. According to the Jews Ishmael was an adult when he was circumcised, while Isaac was still an infant. The baby Isaac, who was miraculously born with the help of the Spirit, was the son of the promise.

Now these Galatians were trying to be circumcised as adults. While they thought they were being obedient by doing it, Paul told them differently. When you volunteer to submit to the law as adults you are not acting like Isaac, the son of the promise. Instead, you are acting like Ishmael, the son of the slave. The Spirit is with the child of the promise, and you are also children of the promise. When you Galatians live according to the law, you remove yourself from the realm of promise and Spirit. In seeking to submit to these Jewish expectations, they were really acting like Ishmael, which would have been seen as a put-down for these believers. This link is not natural to us, but for the early Jewish believers it would have been natural.

The problem now is the same problem that existed then. Living according to the law is easier. There is an unchanging nature to life that exists with the law. One knows what to do, and what not to do. One knows how much weight one can carry, and how many steps to walk on the Sabbath and still be considered faithful to the law. The problem with the law was that it was only meant to tell us when we were wrong, and to condemn those who do the things it prohibits. Which meant that it only served to condemn people, and inevitably to isolate them from those who were keeping that law. Eventually it left Israel frustrated and isolated from the nations around them, and inevitably leaves us isolated from the people around us.

Living by the Spirit is far more difficult in the short term, but far more beneficial in the end. One does not have a written list of expectations to consult, but the continuing presence of God to guide. Knowing what to do requires a continual humility, and the willingness to obey God in every circumstance. The impulse is not what does the law state, but what would God have me do right now? While the law might require us to avoid the person who fails, the Spirit is always searching, always engaging, and always drawing others through a powerful grace. The law puts a fence around the dead areas in our life and tells us to avoid those places. The Spirit renews those areas and brings life. What the law was powerless to do, God did . . . through the Spirit. Sometimes we think that the purpose of Christian faith is to avoid the bad, and to become good. Paul told us something different. The goal of the Christian walk is to experience new life, and that life is given by the Spirit. This is the central truth that energized my friend Paul.

Epilogue
This Is The End

At the end of the book of Acts, Paul was still under house arrest in Rome. We do not know definitively what happened to Paul, as Luke does not tell us. Some say that he died soon after the book of Acts ends. Another strong tradition tells us that Paul was released, and realized his dream of going west to the area he called Spain. I think Paul made it to western Europe and continued his missionary efforts there. If one travels to modern day France and Spain, there are many churches there who claim that their origins go back to Paul's post-Rome journey. After traveling west for a few years, Paul returned to Rome and was arrested and killed by the despotic Nero. I think Paul knew his death was a distinct possibility if he returned to Rome, but he went anyway. Nero needed a scapegoat for the great fire in Rome that some say he started himself, and the Christians would be his target of choice. That did not deter my friend Paul. I wish Acts would have told us about Paul's final days, but the readers of Acts would have known how Paul died, so the author had more important things on his mind. We also tend to forget that the book of Acts was not about Paul, but about how the gospel made it from a manger in Bethlehem to the steps of Rome. When Acts tells us about Paul preaching in Rome, even as he is under house arrest, the book of Acts reaches its climax. The gospel has made its way from a manger to Caesar in about sixty-five years. What a story!

Either way, 2 Timothy finds Paul in captivity and in the final days of his life. There is an intimacy that runs through 2 Timothy that is difficult to miss. As Paul looked back on his life, he stated, "I have run the race. I have kept the faith." As his death loomed ever closer, I am not sure how Paul viewed his life. The staying power of the faith Paul brought to the Roman Empire certainly still hung in the balance. Many of his churches had already failed, and Christians were under intense attack in Rome. I am sure there were dark moments where Paul would have loved to see more evidence of success. The personal faith that Paul kept was a far different one than the one he had followed in his younger years. Paul was still the same man in many ways. He was passionate and faithful before what happened on the road, and he was just as passionate after his life-altering experience on the road. Yet everything had changed, and Paul spent the rest of his life trying to figure out how everything was different and spread that change in town after town.

More than perhaps anyone else at the time, the youthful Paul had remained faithful to the law. Yet his life had changed, and that change had nothing to do with the written code. He had kept the law perfectly and still found himself no closer to God. It had all been a fruitless pursuit. Then Damascus Road happened, and Paul subsequently saw others experience what he had, and many of those others were gentiles. Both he and these gentile believers experienced a life changing faith that was centered around the Spirit, and not the law. At first Paul struggled, and even despaired over this change. How could his beloved law be so worthless? Then Paul began to see that what was happening was not alien to his Judaism, but had been the intention all along. The gentiles were supposed to be a part of God's family, the law had a role, but it was just not the role he had originally envisioned. Paul's life strangely followed his unfolding realization about the law. He had started his life as a zealous believer in exclusive Jewish identity and ended his life writing letters to gentile believers around the empire. His life was not a successful life as most would define it. It started with promise, flourished into leadership at a young age, only to fall back into conflict with the authorities and prison sentence after prison sentence. His life ended with a sentence carried out by a member of the same army he delivered tents to in his youth. Hopefully this book honors my friend Paul, and helps others see what Paul started to see two thousand years ago.

At the end of his life, Paul was mainly alone. Many of the churches he had founded had turned against him and had believed the opponents that followed Paul. Yet there was frequently news about churches that stayed faithful, and some new churches started by others, so there was always hope. Toward the end Paul lived in enforced solitude, with just a few close associates remaining faithful. Paul had spent the last twenty years of his life engaged in the arena of ideas, and his arena was the breadth of the Roman Empire. Now his arena was limited to the square footage of a residence. I think there were days of deep doubt for Paul and he wondered if his efforts had been wasted. He had spent a lifetime spreading his faith, and at times he felt he had little to show for it. As Paul looked at his life and claimed that he had kept the faith, he realized the faith he kept looked a little different. This faith was not centered upon the law anymore, but the indwelling presence of the Holy Spirit. Because of this nothing will ever be the same again, and my friend Paul told us why.

www.ingramcontent.com/pod-product-compliance
Lightning Source LLC
Chambersburg PA
CBHW070738030726
47601CB00001B/59